OPERA

WHAT'S ALL THE SCREAMING ABOUT?

The incomparable grand staircase of the Paris Opéra.

OPERA

WHAT'S ALL THE SCREAMING ABOUT?

ROGER ENGLANDER

WALKER AND COMPANY ❈ NEW YORK

Text copyright © 1983 by Roger Englander
Compact disc ℗ 1964 EMI Records, Ltd.,
    © 1994 by Walker and Company

First published in the United States of America
in 1983 by Walker Publishing Company, Inc.;
first paperback edition published in 1994.

Published simultaneously in Canada by John Wiley & Sons
Canada, Limited, Markham, Ontario.

Library of Congress Cataloging-in-Publication Data
Englander, Roger.
    Opera: what's all the screaming about?
    Bibliography: p.
    Includes index.
    Summary: Traces the development of opera, presents
plots of fifty popular operas, and provides an in-depth
study of "Carmen." Includes lists of composers and their
works, opera companies, opera terms, etc.
    1. Opera—History and criticism—Juvenile literature.
2. Bizet, Georges, 1838–1875. Carmen—Juvenile literature.
[1. Opera—History and criticism. 2. Bizet, Georges, 1838–1875. Carmen] I. Title.
ML1700.E55 1983   782.1   82-23742
ISBN 0-8027-6491-6
ISBN 0-8027-7416-4 (paper)
ISBN 0-8027-7443-1 (paper/CD edition)

Book design by Robert Galster

Printed in the United States of America

10 9 8 7 6 5 4 3

This book is
affectionately
dedicated
to
those three in my life
who were
born on the 25th of August

PICTURE CREDITS

ACKNOWLEDGMENTS

This book came about in all innocence. There are friends, both old and new, I must acknowledge for their roles in its unfolding. It all started with an old friend, Ellen L. Bernstein, who invited me to lecture on "Opera" in her series at Fairfield University in Connecticut. Then Jerome Agel, a colleague and one of the leaders of that new breed of "book producers," asked if he might show the outline of the course to several publishers. And that's where my new friends came in: the editor Jeanne Gardner, together with Sam and Beth Walker (whose publishing company hosts great St. Patrick's Day parties) gave me the go-ahead. Faced with an unaccustomed-to but temporary career, I spent many editing sessions at Jeanne and Richard Gardner's quiet house and glade on the Hudson River, where Jeanne's gourmet lunches sustained us, and introduced me to ceviche, peach chutney, apricot tea, and delicious apples from their own trees.

Encouragement in this first book venture came from my oldest friends, Mark and Joan Malkovich and their children, Mark Jr., Erik, Kent, Kara (and Bonzer), at whose rambling Newport,

Rhode Island, house I actually put pencil to paper. Other true allies, Roberta and George Gaal and Jean Cooke Cavrell, advised me during the decision-making times; and my stalwart protégé, John Bayless, humored me during the trying times.

Completely guileless in their help were other old friends, Harold Gomeau, Betty Stearns, John Walker, and Harry Kraut of Amberson Video. And there were helpful moments from Joe Machlis, John Mauceri, the music and television staff at Indiana University, and the librarian at the Redwood Library in Newport. New acquaintances, Robert Yohn, introduced me to the wonders of computer word processing, and Julie Glass' copy editing skills opened my eyes to the creativity of that calling.

Saving the best for last, I thank the first person I met on my arrival in New York City many years ago, Robert Galster, who aided me in so many ways throughout this project, and then agreed to put his designing talents to work in the look of the book. Through the collaboration of all of the above innocents, my first experience has become a happy one.

CONTENTS

The jewelbox theater of the Altes Residenz, the Cuvilliés in Munich, scene of the world premiere of Mozart's *Idomeneo* in 1781, conducted by the composer himself.

A NOTE FROM
THE AUTHOR

I saw my first opera when I was eight. It was Verdi's *Il Trovatore*, sung in Italian in Cleveland, Ohio. My piano teacher had asked my parents if she could take me. I didn't know anything about the story or the music. I certainly didn't understand the language, but I must have loved it all, especially "Stride la vampa!" and the "Anvil Chorus." I can still remember that I was enthralled for days. I wanted to go right back and see it all over again.

A few months later the Metropolitan Opera Company made its annual visit to Cleveland, and I saw Wagner's masterpiece, *Tristan und Isolde*. Though long and static, it held me spellbound. Opera had become my passion. My early exposure to the giants Verdi and Wagner led me to look forward to the Met's annual spring visits. I found out that I could be an usher in the cavernous auditorium and see eight different operas in one week. By the age of fifteen, I had heard such internationally acclaimed singers as Elisabeth Rethberg and Ezio Pinza, Grace Moore and Jussi Björling, Kirsten Flagstad and Lauritz Melchior.

Later, while I was a student at the University of Chicago, I ushered during seasons of the Chicago Opera Company. By seeing each opera several times, I was able to learn the plots and know the characters.

Fortunately, opera in the United States was breaking out of its traditional mold and reaching a wider audience. Blue-collar workers, salespeople, and students now sat in the large halls and mingled in the foyer with the expensively dressed patrons who had long been opera's principal supporters.

Of course, Donizetti's *Lucia di Lammermoor* was still being sung in Italian, Wagner's *Der Fliegende Holländer* in German, and Offenbach's *Les Contes d'Hoffmann* in French. I had to study an English translation of the plot beforehand to get the full effect of the initial performance. Why, I asked myself, couldn't all opera be sung in English? Everyone in American audiences could then understand the jokes in Mozart's *Le Nozze di Figaro,* and the irony of unrequited love in Massenet's *Manon.*

I began to think about making musical theater my career. I could play several instruments: trumpet, French horn, and piano. I had studied composition with one of the twentieth century's musical giants, Arnold Schoenberg, and had been fortunate in meeting three others—Sergei Rachmaninoff, Igor Stravinsky, and Aaron Copland. More than anything, I wanted to become the conductor of an orchestra. I had conducted the band and the orchestra in high school, but I also wanted to compose music and be involved with the theater.

A standing ovation greeted the artists at the American premiere of *Peter Grimes* at Tanglewood in 1946. Left to right: composer Benjamin Britten (in white jacket), stage director Eric Crozier (smiling), conductor Leonard Bernstein (in profile, in white jacket), and principal singers and chorus.

By chance, on a train from Chicago to Cleveland, I sat next to Erich Leinsdorf, then conductor of the Cleveland Orchestra. His fascinating stories about his work with music made the long trip seem short. I told him about my interest in music, theater, design, and dance, and asked him how I could best use all these interests when I finished college. His reply was direct and unhesitating. "You should become a stage director in opera," he said.

So during my last semester at the university, I applied to the Chicago Opera Company and was given the splendid job of assistant to Fausto Cleva, the artistic director. While working with him, I had the rare opportunity to assist such legendary conductors as Bruno Walter, Fritz Stiedry, Nicolas Rescigno, and Erich Leinsdorf himself.

After graduation, I was invited by Herbert Graf, chief stage director of the Metropolitan Opera Company, to become his assistant for the American premiere of Benjamin Britten's opera, *Peter Grimes*. It was to be performed at Tanglewood, the sum-

mer home of the Boston Symphony Orchestra, and it was to be conducted by Leonard Bernstein, who was twenty-eight years old at the time.

Peter Grimes is powerful theater. It tells the story of a lonely fisherman who has to protect himself from the insults and prejudices of his neighbors, who don't understand his way of life. His frustration and rage drive him to madness—and ultimately to suicide. The impact of the story and music has earned Peter Grimes a place in the standard repertory of opera houses throughout the world. It was my introduction to opera as theater that is relevant to human experience. Every time I see Peter Grimes, I am still moved.

In 1947, while working for a television station in Philadelphia, I produced the first operas ever to be telecast. They were seen over the entire NBC television network—on eight stations from Boston to Richmond. I selected The Medium and The Telephone, two short operas by Gian Carlo Menotti, with whom I had worked in Chicago. He invited me to become his assistant and to restage his works, including The Old Maid and the Thief, Amahl and the Night Visitors, and The Consul. Some were produced on Broadway.

When I produced Menotti's The Old Maid and the Thief for the NBC Opera Company, I was so naive that I didn't realize that live material has to be timed to the second. When the opera was over, I saw that we still had three minutes to fill. Desperately, I signaled to the conductor of the orchestra, and he started to play the overture again. We came out right on the button.

If live theater was often full of unexpected excitement, television was even more so. It was a brand-new medium, with room for all kinds of experimentation. I became an associate director at ABC, assisting on full-length dramas, variety shows, quiz programs, and educational series. When I moved to CBS as a producer and director, I was able to suggest the types of pro-

Gian Carlo Menotti, who wrote words and music for some of the most widely performed operas of the twentieth century.

grams I wanted to produce and direct. Among these were the *New York Philharmonic Young People's Concerts*, which were telecast for eighteen years with Leonard Bernstein and Michael Tilson Thomas as hosts; the long-awaited return to the concert stage of pianist Vladimir Horowitz; a series of events with the world's greatest instrumentalists, *S. Hurok Presents*; the *Bell Telephone Hour*; and *Omnibus*.

I also directed many programs of opera—not full-length, for that would have been too daring, but selected scenes from established and specially commissioned works.

15

Conductor Leonard Bernstein and the author
in a pre-telecast conference for the television series
The New York Philharmonic Young People's Concerts.

Eager to help create new works for the new medium, I proposed the first American opera to be commissioned for television, asking the young composer Lukas Foss (who had never written an opera) to collaborate with the poet Jean Karsavina on *The Jumping Frog of Calaveras County*, a short story by Mark Twain. And from time to time I had the opportunity to direct live musical theater productions in New York, such as Aaron Copland's *The Second Hurricane*, Leonard Bernstein's

Candide, new American operas for the Little Orchestra Society, short scenes for the New York Philharmonic's Promenade Concerts with Andre Kostelanetz, and some obscure early American operas for the Newport Music Festival. Walking to the New York City Center one morning, I heard someone singing "Ridi, Pagliaccio" loud and clear. The impressive voice belonged to a middle-aged, pleasant-looking street singer, who was collecting coins from the apartment dwellers above him and from passersby. I was excited by the quality of his voice and made a point of walking on his street the following week to confirm my first impression. One day I asked him if he had ever sung professionally. He hadn't. I suggested an audition. He appeared exactly on time at the stage door of the New York City Opera Company. László Hálasz, general director of the company, and several of his assistants were eager to hear the singer. A pianist was ready with the *I Pagliacci* score.

My discovery turned into one of the biggest disappointments of my young career. The "important" voice was actually very ordinary without the reverberations from the canyonlike walls of the office and apartment buildings. A nice voice, but not for the opera stage. I learned that what works on the pavement doesn't always work in the theater.

I learned another lesson while staging a production of Bizet's *Carmen* for the New York City Opera. It had fine new costumes and scenery, truckloads of steps and platforms and multilevel playing areas. It also had a very large chorus and ballet corps and many supernumeraries. The leading singers were so internationally mixed that few spoke the same language. The dress rehearsal, at which the entire cast assembled on stage for the first time with sets, costumes, and full orchestra, had been scheduled for only a three-hour period because of a tight budget. The opera runs *three and a half hours*. So we saw only two of the four acts on stage before opening night. The audience

17

had to sit through two acts that had never been fully rehearsed. I promised myself that never again would I stage a live opera without sufficient rehearsal time.

The opera world is much different today than when my interest in it began. Today, an eight-year-old doesn't need a piano teacher to take him to the opera. He need only turn on a television set to see productions from all over the world.

PROLOGUE

The Origins of Opera

Okay, what is opera?

Opera is a story told in singing. It is the amalgam of many arts: theater, music, dance, and design. It has roots in ancient Greek theater, but opera as we know it today was begun four hundred years ago in Florence by a group of intellectual artists attempting to recapture the glory of Greek drama in stories based on the lives of the gods and of royalty. Some early Italian composers were Jacopo Peri, Count Giovanni Bardi, Giulio Caccini, and Vincenzo Galilei (the father of the astronomer Galileo), Florentine collaborators known as the *Camerata* (meaning "a roomful of friends"). Their works were performed only in royal palaces for kings and queens and noble members of the court.

Opera blossomed in the genius of Claudio Monteverdi, whose sublime music is popular to this day. Popes and cardinals began commissioning operas. These were extravagant productions with spectacular stagecraft. Transported to Venice, opera took hold as never before. Surprisingly, the nobles allowed ordinary people to sit in the audience, opera's first democratization. Within a short time, Venice had over a dozen opera houses, theaters built expressly for the purpose of staging and viewing opera.

The themes of these early operas were serious, as some of their titles reveal: *The Drama of the Soul and the Body*, *The Sacrifice of Abraham*, *The Apotheosis of Cephalus*, *The Return of Ulysses to His Country*.

The music was melodic, and accompaniment was sometimes left to the discretion of the musicians, who would "fill in" from suggested harmonies. Usually the orchestra was limited to a small group of string players.

Gradually the lofty themes of royal productions gave way to less weighty subject matter. Comedy was introduced. The seventeenth-century composers Alessandro Scarlatti and Jean-Baptiste Lully developed new forms that were considered quite daring.

It was Wolfgang Amadeus Mozart, in collaboration with the librettist Lorenzo Da Ponte, who took the next giant step forward in popularizing opera by introducing everyday characters. Until this development operatic characters had been kings and queens, gods and goddesses. If a story called for a servant to appear on stage, he never spoke or sang; he merely served.

But in the opera *Le Nozze di Figaro (The Marriage of Figaro)*, based on a revolutionary French play by Pierre-Augustin de

TOP
An eighteenth-century composer contemplates the many imaginary characters he has created for the French opera stage.

BOTTOM
A French impresario "counting the house" before the curtain (and the chandeliers) rises on a seventeenth-century opera performance in Paris.

Beaumarchais, servants were the principal singing characters. Italian audiences laughed when they heard the native dialogue sung by Figaro and Susanna. Only a few years before, the idea of servants in the roles of hero and heroine had caused the original play to be banned from many European stages. The addition of orchestral music and the passing of time had helped to create a more receptive atmosphere.

The tunes of early operas and *singspiels* (music with spoken dialogue) became as familiar in the streets of Vienna, Prague, and Paris as the Broadway show tunes and lyrics of George and Ira Gershwin, Cole Porter, and Frank Loesser would become in New York two centuries later.

Through the works of Mozart, Richard Wagner, and Charles Gounod, opera spread outward from Italy until every major European city had its opera house, usually in the very center of town. They were theaters with stage machinery so elaborate

A *plain* opera house in America: the New Chestnut Street Theater in Philadelphia, where opera was performed in 1825.

A *fancy* opera house in Europe: The Vienna Opera in the center of the city of Haydn, Mozart, Schubert, and Beethoven.

and theatrical effects so complex that much of today's theater technology seems primitive by comparison. They were the *Star Wars* of their day. It is an interesting fact that the proscenium, the arch that frames the stage, was introduced in an Italian *opera* house in Parma to mask the quantity of backstage machinery that produced these stupendous effects.

The first musical theater piece to be performed in the New World was entitled *Flora, or Hob in the Well*. The year was 1735, and the community was Charles Town, South Carolina. Sixty years later, the young American nation saw its first opera—*Tammany*, by James Hewitt. *Leonora*, the first grand opera written by an American composer, William Henry Fry, was produced in 1845.

Twenty years later, at the end of the Civil War, the first American musical comedy was produced almost by accident. A New York entrepreneur had imported from France a troupe of bal-

let dancers, who arrived with numerous elaborate stage sets. But before the production opened, the theater burned to the ground. The only other New York stage big enough to hold the extravagant scenic effects was already engaged for a melodrama called *The Black Crook*. The two shows joined forces. They mixed the melodramatic scenes with dancing, music, and spectacle. For five and a half hours nightly, the audience was enthralled by a new entertainment. The show was a hit, playing 474 performances.

When European operatic masterpieces were imported, they were performed in jewelbox theaters seating only a few hundred of the wealthiest members of society in such cultural centers as New Orleans, New York, and Philadelphia. Italian, French, and German operas were sung in their original languages by singers from Europe. It was not until the mid-nineteenth century that American audiences were treated to an occasional American singer—trained in Europe, of course. Only much later was any English translation of a well-known opera performed.

These rare translations, however, were hard to follow. Excessively flowery language obscured the meaning, and the singers' English diction was not always clear.

Certain elitist groups of opera fans still decry English translations. Others cling to such outmoded traditions as the Monday night subscription series, where reserved seats are passed down from father to son, and where it is *de rigueur* for men to wear black tie and women their diamond chokers on opening night. Still others want opera produced as if it were untouchable, raised on a pedestal. Such customs may help to perpetuate the mystique of opera, but they add little to its enjoyment. In fact, these stodgy conventions turn some people away from opera.

Certainly, knowledgeable operagoers receive greater pleasure from a performance than do neophytes. It is not essential, however, to know all the ramifications of the story of an opera in order to become interested in it. Following are the plots of fifty popular operas, reduced to their bare bones and presented as if they were modern-day news events told in banner headlines. They capture the essence of what you need to know.

LOVERS BURIED ALIVE IN TOMB AS JILTED PRINCESS MOURNS

Aida

Music: Giuseppe Verdi   Libretto: Antonio Ghislanzoni, in Italian
First performance: Cairo, December 24, 1871

GOVERNOR ASSASSINATED BY BEST FRIEND AT FANCY DRESS BALL

Un Ballo in Maschera (*A Masked Ball*)

Music: Giuseppe Verdi   Libretto: Antonio Somma, in Italian
First performance: Rome, February 17, 1859

MAY/DECEMBER MARRIAGE THWARTED BY DISGUISED NOBLEMAN

Il Barbiere di Siviglia (*The Barber of Seville*)

Music: Gioacchino Rossini
Libretto: Cesare Sterbini, after Pierre-Augustin de Beaumarchais, in Italian
First performance: Rome, February 20, 1816

SEAMSTRESS COUGHS TO DEATH AS FRIENDS LOOK ON

La Bohème (*Bohemian Life*)

Music: Giacomo Puccini
Libretto: Giuseppe Giacosa and Luigi Illica, after Henri Murger, in Italian
First performance: Turin, February 1, 1896

MURDEROUS RUSSIAN LEADER GOES MAD; PROCLAIMS SON SUCCESSOR TO FALSE THRONE

Boris Godunov

Music: Modest Mussorgsky
Libretto by the composer, after Alexander Pushkin, in Russian
First performance: St. Petersburg, February 8, 1874

AWOL SOLDIER KNIFES LOVER OUTSIDE BULLRING WHILE CROWD CHEERS MATADOR

Carmen

Music: Georges Bizet
Libretto: Henri Meilhac and Ludovic Halévy, after Prosper Mérimée, in French
First performance: Paris, March 3, 1875

EASTER FESTIVITIES END IN MURDER AFTER MAN IS BITTEN ON EAR

Cavalleria Rusticana (*Rustic Chivalry*)

Music: Pietro Mascagni
Libretto: Guido Menasci and Giovanni Targioni-Tozzetti,
after Giovanni Verga, in Italian
First performance: Rome, May 17, 1890

UNDERGROUND SPY'S UNANSWERED PHONE CALL TRIGGERS ILL-TIMED SUICIDE

The Consul

Music: Gian Carlo Menotti   Libretto by the composer, in English
First performance: Philadelphia, March 1, 1950

WRITER/HERO'S THREE ROMANCES NIPPED IN THE BUD BY EVIL MAGICIAN

Les Contes d'Hoffmann (*The Tales of Hoffmann*)
Music: Jacques Offenbach
Libretto: Jules Barbier and Michel Carré, after E. T. A. Hoffmann, in French
First performance: Paris, February 10, 1881

SWEET-TALKING CYNIC TEMPTS GIRLS TO SWITCH LOVERS

Così fan Tutte (*They All Do It*, or *The School for Lovers*)
Music: Wolfgang Amadeus Mozart   Libretto: Lorenzo Da Ponte, in Italian
First performance: Vienna, January 26, 1790

STATUE DRAGS RAKE TO HELL AS COUNTLESS BEAUTIES MOURN

Don Giovanni (*Don Juan*)
Music: Wolfgang Amadeus Mozart
Libretto: Lorenzo Da Ponte, in Italian
First performance: Prague, October 29, 1787

CAPTURED MAIDENS RESCUED FROM TURKISH HAREM

Die Entführung aus dem Serail (*The Abduction from the Seraglio*)
Music: Wolfgang Amadeus Mozart   Libretto: Gottlieb Stephanie, in German
First performance: Vienna, July 16, 1782

DUEL TO THE DEATH WAGED OVER WOMAN'S FAVOR

Eugene Onegin

Music: Peter Ilyich Tchaikovsky

Libretto by the composer and K. S. Shilovsky, after Alexander Pushkin,
in Russian

First performance: Moscow, March 29, 1879

FAT KNIGHT WASHED UP BY WILY WIVES

Falstaff

Music: Giuseppe Verdi

Libretto: Arrigo Boito, after William Shakespeare, in Italian

First performance: Milan, February 9, 1893

PHILOSOPHER SELLS OUT TO DEVIL; WIFE GOES TO HEAVEN

Faust

Music: Charles Gounod

Libretto: Jules Barbier and Michel Carré, after Johann Wolfgang von Goethe,
in French

First performance: Paris, March 19, 1859

DEVOTED WIFE PLANS JAIL BREAK FOR WRONGED SPOUSE

Fidelio

Music: Ludwig van Beethoven

Libretto: Josef Sonnleithner, in German

First performance: Vienna, November 20, 1805

PHILANDERING HUSBAND LANDS IN SLAMMER DUPED BY WIFE AND MAID

Die Fledermaus (*The Bat*)

Music: Johann Strauss

Libretto: Carl Haffner and Richard Genée, after Henri Meilhac and Ludovic Halévy,
in German

First performance: Vienna, April 5, 1874

FATHER'S CURSE TRIGGERS EVENTS RESULTING IN CHILDREN'S DEATHS

La Forza del Destino (*The Force of Destiny*)
Music: Giuseppe Verdi   Libretto: Francesco Piave, in Italian
First performance: St. Petersburg, November 10, 1862

VENETIAN CANALS SPEW CORPSES AS STREET SINGER COMPLICATES MANY LIVES

La Gioconda (*The Joyful Girl*)
Music: Amilcare Ponchielli
Libretto: Arrigo Boito (Tobia Gorrio), after Victor Hugo, in Italian
First performance: Milan, April 8, 1876

LOST CHILDREN SEND CAPTOR TO A GINGERBREAD FATE

Hänsel und Gretel
Music: Engelbert Humperdinck
Libretto: Adelheid Wette, after the Brothers Grimm, in German
First performance: Weimar, December 23, 1893

FAITHFUL BRIDE'S DISGUISED BROTHER RESCUED; GROOM DISAPPEARS ON WEDDING NIGHT

Lohengrin
Music: Richard Wagner   Libretto by the composer, in German
First performance: Weimar, August 28, 1850

SPRINGTIME IN PARIS: SCENE OF COUPLE'S FORBIDDEN ELOPEMENT

Louise
Music: Gustave Charpentier   Libretto by the composer, in French
First performance: Paris, February 2, 1900

BRIDE GOES MAD;
MURDERS HUSBAND ON WEDDING NIGHT

Lucia di Lammermoor

Music: Gaetano Donizetti

Libretto: Salvatore Cammarano, based on Sir Walter Scott, in Italian

First performance: Naples, September 26, 1835

JILTED IN ARRANGED MARRIAGE;
WIFE DESTROYS SELF

Madama Butterfly

Music: Giacomo Puccini

Libretto: Giuseppe Giacosa and Luigi Illica, after David Belasco, in Italian

First performance: Milan, February 17, 1904

DEAD IN LOVER'S ARMS;
EXILED COURTESAN MISSES BOAT

Manon

Music: Jules Massenet

Libretto: Henri Meilhac and Philippe Gille, after Abbé Prévost, in French

First performance: Paris, January 19, 1884

FRENCH BEAUTY EXILED
TO LIFE ON AMERICAN DESERT

Manon Lescaut

Music: Giacomo Puccini

Libretto: Ruggiero Leoncavallo, Marco Praga, Domenico Oliva, Giuseppe Giacosa, Giulio Ricordi, and Luigi Illica, after Abbé Prévost, in Italian

First performance: Turin, February 1, 1893

NEW BOY IN TOWN WINS GIRL
AND CONTEST WITH HEAVENLY SONG

Die Meistersinger von Nürnberg (*The Mastersingers of Nuremberg*)
Music: Richard Wagner   Libretto by the composer, in German
First performance: Munich, June 21, 1868

CRAZED DO-GOODER TORCHES CASTLE;
FULFILLS ROMANCE FOR LONG-LOST DAUGHTER

Mignon
Music: Ambroise Thomas
Libretto: Jules Barbier and Michel Carré, after Johann Wolfgang von Goethe,
in French
First performance: Paris, November 17, 1866

PAGAN PRIESTESS DIES
WITH LOVER ON FLAMING PYRE

Norma
Music: Vincenzo Bellini   Libretto: Felice Romani, in Italian
First performance: Milan, December 26, 1831

NOBLEMAN ESCAPES NET OF INTRIGUE
WOVEN BY WIFE AND LOYAL SERVANTS

Le Nozze di Figaro (*The Marriage of Figaro*)
Music: Wolfgang Amadeus Mozart
Libretto: Lorenzo Da Ponte, after Pierre-Augustin de Beaumarchais, in Italian
First performance: Vienna, May 1, 1786

JEALOUS HUSBAND STRANGLES INNOCENT WIFE

Otello
Music: Giuseppe Verdi
Libretto: Arrigo Boito, after William Shakespeare, in Italian
First performance: Milan, February 5, 1887

CLOWN KNIFES TWO-TIMING WIFE IN REAL-LIFE DRAMA

I Pagliacci (*The Clowns*)
Music: Ruggiero Leoncavallo
Libretto by the composer, in Italian
First performance: Milan, May 21, 1892

GRAIL LEADER'S WOUNDS HEALED BY PERFECT KNIGHT

Parsifal
Music: Richard Wagner   Libretto by the composer, in German
First performance: Bayreuth, July 26, 1882

LONG-HAIRED BEAUTY SETS BROTHER AGAINST BROTHER

Pelléas et Mélisande
Music: Claude Debussy
Libretto: Maurice Maeterlinck, in French
First performance: Paris, April 30, 1902

ACCUSED FISHERMAN DROWNS TO ESCAPE PUNISHMENT

Peter Grimes
Music: Benjamin Britten
Libretto: Montagu Slater, after George Crabbe, in English
First performance: London, June 7, 1945

ISLAND PICNIC LEADS WEAK WOMAN TO DRUGS AND BIG-CITY LIFE

Porgy and Bess
Music: George Gershwin
Libretto: DuBose Heyward and Ira Gershwin, in English
First performance: Boston, September 30, 1935

BOHEMIAN LAD FINDS NEW WIFE AND PARENTS ON SAME DAY

Prodaná nevěsta (The Bartered Bride)
Music: Bedřich Smetana   Libretto: Karel Sabina, in Czech
First performance: Prague, May 30, 1866

COURT JESTER'S DAUGHTER FOUND MURDERED; FATHER LEFT HOLDING THE BAG

Rigoletto
Music: Giuseppe Verdi
Libretto: Francesco Piave, after Victor Hugo, in Italian
First performance: Venice, March 11, 1851

DWARF STEALS GOLD. BROTHER WEDS SISTER. BEAUTY AWAKENS WITH A KISS. HERO'S DEATH BRINGS DOOMSDAY.

Der Ring des Nibelungen (The Ring of the Nibelungs)
Music: Richard Wagner   Libretto by the composer, in German
First Performance:
Das Rheingold (The Rhinegold), Munich, September 22, 1869
Die Walküre (The Valkyrie), Munich, June 26, 1870
Siegfried, Bayreuth, August 16, 1876
Götterdämmerung (The Twilight of the Gods), Bayreuth, August 17, 1876

AGING NOBLEWOMAN BLESSES YOUNGER RIVAL'S NUPTIALS

Der Rosenkavalier (*The Cavalier of the Rose*)
Music: Richard Strauss
Libretto: Hugo von Hofmannsthal, in German
First performance: Dresden, January 26, 1911

PRINCESS' BIZARRE REQUEST BRINGS DEATH CRUSH

Salome
Music: Richard Strauss
Libretto by the composer, after Oscar Wilde, in German
First performance: Dresden, December 9, 1905

STRONG MAN BRINGS DOWN THE HOUSE

Samson et Dalila
Music: Camille Saint-Saëns
Libretto: Ferdinand Lemaire, in French
First performance: Weimar, December 2, 1877

SINGER'S PROFANED LOVE ABSOLVED BY MAIDEN'S FAITH

Tannhäuser
Music: Richard Wagner   Libretto by the composer, in German
First performance: Dresden, October 19, 1845

FAMED ACTRESS STABS POLICE CHIEF; LEAPS TO DEATH

Tosca

Music: Giacomo Puccini
Libretto: Luigi Illica and Giuseppe Giacosa, after Victorien Sardou, in Italian
First performance: Rome, January 14, 1900

MISGUIDED SOCIETY BELLE SUCCUMBS AFTER TOO MANY PARTIES

La Traviata (*The Wayward Woman*)

Music: Giuseppe Verdi
Libretto: Francesco Piave, after Alexandre Dumas, in Italian
First performance: Venice, March 6, 1853

LOVE POTION LEADS TO DOUBLE DEATH

Tristan und Isolde

Music: Richard Wagner   Libretto by the composer, in German
First performance: Munich, June 10, 1865

BABY SWITCH PROVIDES TROUBLE FOR NOBLE FAMILY

Il Trovatore (*The Troubadour*)

Music: Giuseppe Verdi
Libretto: Salvatore Cammarano, in Italian
First performance: Rome, January 19, 1853

PRINCE SOLVES RIDDLES; RISKS LIFE FOR HAND OF PRINCESS

Turandot

Music: Giacomo Puccini

Libretto: Giuseppe Adami and Renato Simoni, after Carlo Gozzi, in Italian

First performance: Milan, April 25, 1926

CRAZED SOLDIER DROWNS AFTER MURDER OF FAITHLESS MISTRESS

Wozzeck

Music: Alban Berg

Libretto by the composer, after Georg Büchner, in German

First performance: Berlin, December 14, 1925

BOY WINS GIRL THROUGH TRIAL OF FIRE AND WATER

Die Zauberflöte (*The Magic Flute*)

Music: Wolfgang Amadeus Mozart

Libretto: Emanuel Schikaneder, in German

First performance: Vienna, September 30, 1791

I have divided the rest of this book into three sections: The Creators, The Interpreters, and The Appreciators. The division was not made for idle love of triptychs, but evolved from my deep conviction that it takes those three units to make music. We, the audience, are an important member of the trio.

In addition to information about opera in general, each section includes a step-by-step account of the creation of one of the world's most popular operas, Georges Bizet's *Carmen*—its inception, some of the creative decisions involved, staging dilemmas, and the theatrical excitement.

Telling a story with words and music is one of the highest forms of art. In opera, it is an art that causes audiences to split into vociferous and sometimes battling camps—the fanatics who yell "Bravo!" after every well-turned phrase of *La Bohème* and those who stay away in droves from what they discern as screaming "Mimis" and "Rodolfos."

What *is* all the screaming about? Read on and find out.

PART ONE

THE
CREATORS

The facade of the Metropolitan Opera House at Lincoln Center, New York City.

1
THE LIBRETTIST

In the Beginning Was the Word

In opera it is the librettist who supplies the words; he is the storyteller. The creation of all operas begins with the story.

We are attracted to good stories. We like to hear them. We like to tell them. Children have always begged for stories. Cave dwellers and hunters sat around camp fires and spun tales of high adventure and narrow escapes. People tell jokes and listen to gossip. They read short stories and novels. They watch soap operas and situation comedies on television. They pay money to watch plays and movies in theaters.

What is so appealing about a story? Most stories are in the past tense, but we live our lives in the present. Things are happening to us every minute, and we cannot predict the outcome. In a story, however, we learn the ending right away.

Every good story has its beginning, middle, and end. A story can entertain, amuse, shock, horrify, or anger. It can influence our lives. We can learn from the mistakes and unfounded fears of storybook characters. Good stories can give us solutions to problems and insights to our emotions.

The stories of popular operas today can be divided into two groups: *tragic* and *comic*. The larger group is the tragic; its plots deal with two basic subjects—love and death. Occasionally a plot centers on jealousy or revenge or a variation on either. But serious opera plots essentially boil down to ''I love you; why don't you love me?'' and ''Too bad that I must die!''—highly emotional themes that lend themselves to musical expression and larger-than-life characters and situations. The second and smaller group, comic plots, are usually based on love, too—love in confusion, love between impossibly paired mates, or love involving disguised suitors who are revealed to each other only at the final curtain. Often the circumstances surrounding these plots spotlight a social situation prevalent at the time the libretto was written. Sometimes they ridicule a particular personality or custom.

In the early history of Italian opera, tragic opera, or *opera seria*, was the principal attraction for the audience. Between the acts, comic *intermezzi* were performed. These had no relationship to the main event; they merely served as diversions. Eventually these short comic sketches became full-length works known as *opera buffa*.

The story line of an opera is created by the *librettist*, the writer of the *libretto*. Libretto is an Italian word meaning ''small book'' (from the Latin *liber*, for ''book''). In early operas, the words were bound into a small booklet, separate from the music. Because it was shorter, the smaller book containing the text was known as the libretto. It forms the spine of the opera and has always been written before the music. Sometimes there is more than one librettist.

42

The *lyricist*, who writes the words to the music, may not be the same person who outlines the drama. Lyricist comes from the Greek noun *lyric*. Its root is *lyre*, a word for the harplike stringed instrument strummed by ancient poet-musicians while they sang or recited. The lyrics of any musical piece are the actual words that the performers sing.

The number of words in an opera is almost always fewer than those in the play on which it is based. If one compares the original text of Shakespeare's *Othello* with Arrigo Boito's libretto for Verdi's opera *Otello* (the Italian spelling), the difference is readily noted.

Two principal problems faced Boito. First, it takes much longer to say anything *with* music than without. Second, simple rather than complex emotions and clearly stated rather than ambiguous problems lend themselves best to musical theater. So Boito had to shorten and simplify the play. He almost completely omitted Shakespeare's first act, he telescoped scenes, he eliminated some characters, and he simplified others. He invented such substitutions as the opening storm scene, which does not appear in the play, adding a great dramatic effect. He also added the "Credo" and the "Ave Maria."

There is one opera where the original text remains intact. The libretto was taken from Oscar Wilde's one-act play *Salome* and made into an opera by Richard Strauss. From the opening lines, "How beautiful is the Princess Salome tonight!" to the closing command, "Kill that woman!", the original text is preserved almost word for word. Naturally, the opera is nearly three times as long as the spoken drama. But when the action stops and the music takes over with its peculiar continuum, real time is suspended.

Language is generally formalized in opera because music has a formal, almost unreal quality of its own. Yet the purpose of using words with music is to celebrate *both* of those forms of expression and to use them each to enhance the other. A weak or

Lorenzo Da Ponte (1749–1838), the librettist of Mozart's *Don Giovanni, The Marriage of Figaro,* and *Così fan Tutte.* (From a painting by Samuel F. B. Morse.)

uninteresting story line simply doesn't work.

Three writers who have contributed outstanding libretti for successful operas are Lorenzo Da Ponte, Arrigo Boito, and Hugo von Hofmannsthal. (A more extensive list of leading librettists may be found in the Appendix, page 167.)

Lorenzo Da Ponte was an Italian, the son of a Jewish leather merchant. Born Emanuele Conegliano, he changed his name when he adopted Christianity and studied for the priesthood. His life outside the church, however, was so full of amorous adventures that he was forced to move from city to city. He finally exiled himself to the United States at the beginning of the nineteenth century and taught Italian at Columbia University, augmenting his income by running a grocery story in Greenwich Village.

44

Arrigo Boito (1842–1918), who wrote the libretti for Ponchielli's *La Gioconda* and Verdi's *Otello* and *Falstaff*, as well as the words and music to his own operas.

As a poet in Vienna, Da Ponte created the *libretti* for Mozart's *Don Giovanni (Don Juan), Così fan Tutte (They All Do It, or The School for Lovers),* and *The Marriage of Figaro,* achievements that insure his immortality and overshadow his colorful other-life.

Don Giovanni has been proclaimed by many as not only the greatest opera ever written, but also one of the greatest achievements in all the arts. There is scarcely a human feeling that is not expressed through its situations or characters. It tells of a libertine (probably patterned after Casanova, a friend and companion of Da Ponte) who woos too many women, entangles himself with the powerful, and is dragged to the depths of Hell.

Arrigo Boito lived in Italy a hundred years ago. Not only did he adapt two Shakespeare plays into libretti of the operas *Otello* and *Falstaff* for the aging and famous composer Giuseppe Verdi, but he was also a composer himself. He wrote the words and music for *Mefistofele* (*Mephisto*) and *Nerone* (*Nero*), operas still performed today throughout the world. For another Italian composer, Amilcare Ponchielli, he wrote the libretto of *La Gioconda* (*The Joyful Girl*) under the pseudonym of Tobia Gorrio, an anagram of his own name.

Boito's libretti for the Verdi operas are universally acclaimed as models of clarity and dramatic variety. Without Boito, Verdi could never have achieved the complete freedom from convention that characterizes his last two operas.

Late in his life, Boito entered politics and was elected to the Roman senate, yet he continued to write his operas.

Hugo von Hofmannsthal was an Austrian poet who had an outstanding career as a playwright before he began his long collaboration with the composer Richard Strauss. He was responsible for the words to *Der Rosenkavalier* (*The Cavalier of the Rose*), *Elektra*, *Arabella*, *Die Frau ohne Schatten* (*The Woman without a Shadow*), and *Ariadne auf Naxos* (*Ariadne of Naxos*). The correspondence between these two artists still survives, offering insight into the problems of libretto writing and the mysteries of the collaborative process.

Der Rosenkavalier, an original story by von Hofmannsthal, is a sentimental, bittersweet tale of an aging but beautiful princess who eventually blesses the fairy-tale union of her former young lover and his even younger bride. It offered Strauss the opportunity to indulge himself in every facet of musical writing from lilting Viennese waltzes to a vocal trio of heavenly beauty.

After World War I, Hofmannsthal co-founded the Salzburg Festival in Austria with the renowned theater and film director Max Reinhardt. Their production of *Everyman* is seen there every summer to this day.

Of the hundreds of opera productions in America, perhaps only twenty percent are performed in English. There are many

Hugo von Hofmannsthal (1874–1929), the librettist
for Richard Strauss's *Der Rosenkavalier, Elektra,*
Ariadne auf Naxos, and *Die Frau ohne Schatten.*

people who contend that "Celeste Aida, forma divina, mistico serto, di luce e fior" sung in English as "Fairest Aida, star of my dreaming, born of the sunlight, bathed by the dew" is not only a sacrilege, but is also unattractive to the ear and ungainly for the voice. There is, however, an acceptable way of freely translating that same phrase into "Heav'nly Aida, beauty resplendent, radiant flower, blooming and bright." It is important that translations retain the most graceful of the singing vowels in their proper place. It is also important that they maintain the spirit, the meaning, and the singing ease of the original language.

A good translation of *La Bohème* (*Bohemian Life*) has been made by Howard Dietz, the Broadway lyricist of *A Tree Grows in Brooklyn*. Other excellent English translations include *Madama Butterfly* by Boris Goldovsky, head of the Curtis Institute of Music's opera department; *Die Entführung aus dem Serail* (*The Abduction from the Seraglio*) by Andrew Porter, music critic for *The New Yorker*; and *Carmen* by Sheldon Harnick, who wrote the lyrics for *Fiddler on the Roof*. The demonstrated worth of such translations into singable English has helped the battle against arguments of purist diehards, who defend the original languages of the old European works.

Many of these same diehards do not even look favorably upon new operas *written* in English. Other than such occasional successes as *Billy Budd* (by the Englishman Benjamin Britten, libretto by the novelist E. M. Forster and Eric Crozier), or *The Medium* (both words and music by the Italian-American Gian Carlo Menotti), or *Porgy and Bess* (by the Brooklyn-born George Gershwin, libretto by DuBose Heyward and lyrics by Ira Gershwin), they contend that English with its hard consonants is a poor choice for singing, especially when compared to Italian with its open vowels.

Rhyme plays an important role in opera lyrics as well as in popular songs. Sometimes a word or phrase of a lyric is missed by the audience; the rhyming word is an insurance that the meaning of the whole phrase is understood. Sometimes an audience can anticipate what words will be sung even before hearing the rhyme. At other times an unexpected rhyme is substituted for something obvious, giving the audience a surprise. The librettist is the most underrated and unacknowledged person in all of opera. Some opera house programs do not even list the names of the librettist and lyricist, and they are almost never printed on posters or in ads.

If singers and concert managers insisted on having the names of both creators printed on their concert programs, the writers of the lyrics would begin to find their valued place in musical history. Writing opera is a collaborative process. Proper credit must be given to Antonio Ghislanzoni, who wrote the words for Aida, to Jules Barbier and Michel Carré for Faust, to Francesco Piave for La Traviata (The Wayward Woman), to Felice Romani for Norma, to Cesare Sterbini for Il Barbiere di Siviglia (The Barber of Seville), and to countless others whose names have faded into oblivion.

In the earliest days of opera, the librettist was given all the credit; the name of the composer was often overlooked or eliminated from publication and announcements. Pietro Metastasio's libretti, for example, were so acclaimed that one of them was set to music by as many as sixty different composers, and Metastasio's name was printed more prominently than theirs. No wonder some composers felt slighted.

But that was over 250 years ago—too long to hold a grudge.

An 1866 photograph of Henri Meilhac (1831–1897)
and (standing) Ludovic Halévy (1834–1908),
librettists for Bizet's *Carmen*.

THE LIBRETTISTS OF CARMEN

To trace the development of one single opera through all of its creative and interpretive stages, I have selected *Carmen*, since it is possibly the most widely performed opera in the world today and, incidentally, one of my favorites. It has also been called "the perfect opera," probably for its ideal blend of drama and music.

The libretto of *Carmen* was written by Henri Meilhac and Ludovic Halévy. Its music was composed by Georges Bizet, who was thirty-five years old when he was commissioned in 1872 to write a full-length work for the Paris Opéra-Comique. Bizet decided to base his work on an actual incident that had been the subject of a popular novel by Prosper Mérimée, published some thirty years earlier. The plot revolved around an attractive gypsy girl named Carmen and her soldier lover, who was jealous of her attentions to other men.

The dramatic and musical possibilities of the story caught Bizet's imagination, and he was given the opportunity to work with two of France's most successful opera librettists, Meilhac and Halévy. Several years older than Bizet, both had worked together on a number of successfully produced libretti for the leading theater composer of Paris, Jacques Offenbach.

Meilhac and Halévy elaborated on the original story, inventing new characters (Micaëla, the sweet and shy country girl), eliminating some (Garcia, Carmen's jealous husband), and changing the names of others and enlarging their importance (Escamillo, the matador, was a mere picador named Lucas in the original). Bizet also contributed significantly to the dramatic structure of the libretto. In fact, he wrote all the words to three of the most famous pieces: the "Habanera," the "Seguidilla," and the "Card Trio."

Not much documentation exists on the writing of Carmen, nor is much known about the collaborative techniques of the two writers, but it is thought that Meilhac, who was more at home with broad humor, probably wrote the spoken dialogue, and that Halévy handled the sentimental sections and most of the musical verse.

Bizet's choice of Carmen as a subject met with many objections from the opera managers who had commissioned him to write it. When Halévy was asked by the head of the Opéra to report on their progress, he was warned that everyone would be horrified at such a subject. "Mérimée's Carmen?" said the director. "Isn't she killed by her lover? I won't have that despicable background of thieves, gypsies, and cigarmakers at the Opéra-Comique, a family theater! Marriages are arranged here! Boxes are booked for courting. You'll frighten off our audience! It's impossible."

Halévy explained that the subject would be softened, that "a very innocent, very chaste young girl" would be introduced. Yes, he admitted, there were gypsies, but *comic* gypsies. As for the death scene, it would be "sneaked in at the end of a very lively, very brilliant act, played in bright sunlight on a holiday with triumphal processions, ballets, and joyous fanfares." As Halévy left the office, the director pleaded, "Please try not to have her die. Death on the stage of the Opéra-Comique! Such a thing has never been seen! Never! Don't make her die. I beg you."

Both Halévy and Meilhac were such popular and successful librettists that they attended only three of the rehearsals of *Carmen*. They had four other shows running concurrently in the music halls of Paris, and *Carmen*, even though it was their first work to appear at the Opéra-Comique, was simply another show. Halévy wrote shortly before the opening, "I hope for a happy evening for Bizet. The thing has little importance for Meilhac and me."

SYNOPSIS OF THE PLOT

The prelude to *Carmen* sets the scene. The vigorous first theme in the orchestra suggests a gathering of a boisterous crowd ready to enjoy the spectacle of a bullfight. The melody of the "Toreador Song" is briefly interjected, and the bustling music of the crowd returns, but the prelude is not over. In a surprise turn, Bizet continues "scene painting" with a sudden change of musical events. In a minor key, mysterious and full of impending doom, underlying tragedy is suggested.

The curtain rises on the public square in Seville. Townspeople mill about on their daily rounds, sellers and buyers make deals, children play in the streets, and there are soldiers on duty. A young girl, Micaëla, asks where she might find her childhood friend, José. She is new to the town and has come with a message from his mother. She is told that José is expected to resume guard duty at any moment.

The tobacco factory has just closed for a midday break. The men of the town gather to wait for their favorite cigarette maker, the attractive and flirtatious gypsy, Carmen. Singing the "Habanera," Carmen states her philosophy of love—to be free as a bird, and not to be forced. "When you love me," she says, "I can't love you, so it's very dangerous to love me." The meaning of these words foretells the end of the story.

As Carmen returns to work, she sees the soldier, José, and throws him a flower to attract his attention. Micaëla returns to give José greetings from home; he remembers that sometime in the near future he will probably marry this sweet childhood friend.

Suddenly there is a disturbance in the factory. Carmen has caused a fight among her co-workers. The square fills with squabbling women, and the soldiers are called to restore peace. Carmen is given over to José, who must tie her hands to quiet her. She whispers to him that if he allows her to escape, she will see him that evening at a neighboring tavern. Singing a seductive aria, the "Seguidilla," she is persuasive enough to get loose, push José to the ground, and run away laughing as the curtain falls.

A short orchestral prelude precedes Act II, which takes place in the tavern of Lillas Pastia, a meeting place for smugglers and gypsies. A wild "Gypsy Dance" is in progress, and Carmen and her friends, Frasquita and Mercédès, join in. A group of sports

The public square in Seville, scene of the first act of *Carmen* in a production staged at Indiana University School of Music, Bloomington, in 1978.

The tavern of Lillas Pastia, the second act of *Carmen* performed at Indiana University.

fans enter with their hero, Escamillo, the most popular matador in Spain. As he sings the "Toreador Song," he and Carmen find themselves attracted to one another.

After Escamillo leaves, a quartet of smugglers tells Carmen of their plan to leave that evening for the mountains. They need her help to distract the guards while they carry stolen goods across the border. Carmen doesn't want to join them because she is waiting for José.

When José arrives, she dances for him alone, true to her promise. José confesses his interest in her, but says he cannot stay because the bugle has sounded retreat and he must return to the barracks. This angers Carmen, who feels rejected. José sings the romantic "Flower Song," in which he tells Carmen that the blossom she had tossed to him enabled him to tolerate the harsh punishment he received as a result of her escape.

They are interrupted by José's commanding officer, Zuniga, who hopes to romance Carmen himself. The two soldiers engage in a duel. José's challenge to his lieutenant is an act of insubordination that seals his fate. Zuniga leaves, unharmed but humiliated, and José has no choice but to desert the army and go off to the mountains with Carmen and her smuggler friends. The act ends with a chorus in praise of freedom and liberty.

Act III opens with an orchestral prelude that paints the serene picture of night in the mountain camp. The smugglers have gathered their consignment of stolen goods and are resting before crossing into the rugged border country. To pass the time, the women tell fortunes with cards. Carmen joins them to deal her own fortune and, in the "Card Trio," clearly reads her own fate: death at the hands of a rejected lover.

The mountain camp of the gypsy smugglers in the third act of
Carmen as staged at Indiana University. The musicians are seen in
the orchestra pit below the stage.

They all depart for the border, leaving José to guard the camp. Micaëla appears in the shadows with a guide and sings a haunting aria describing her fright at being left alone in such a desolate place. While she hides, the matador Escamillo appears. He has come to find Carmen. Seeing him, José draws his dagger. Carmen and the other gypsies rush in to stop the fight and save Escamillo from being overcome by José. Micaëla is discovered crouching behind a rock, and tells José that she brings the sad message that his mother is dying. In disgust over Carmen's attraction to Escamillo, which is now very evident, he throws the gypsy to the ground as he leaves with Micaëla. The tragedy suggested in the opening prelude is now beginning to take shape.

The orchestral prelude to Act IV reflects the bustle of holiday crowds. The scene takes place outside the bullring. The procession of contestants and spectators arrives—the toreros, the ban-

Outside the bullring near Seville in the fourth
act of Indiana University's staging of *Carmen.*

derilleros, the picadors, and finally Escamillo himself, accompanied by Carmen.

The crowd disperses, leaving Carmen alone with her gypsy friends, Frasquita and Mercédès, who warn her that José has returned and is lurking nearby. Carmen proudly states that she is unafraid and is ready to meet and challenge what she knows is her fate.

José, ragged and miserable, enters and confronts Carmen. Does she love him or the matador? During their argument, Carmen takes the ring that José had given her and throws it to the ground. Jealous and angered, José tries to keep Carmen from entering the bullring, where the crowds are cheering Escamillo's victory. The only way to stop her is with his knife. He stabs her with the drawn blade. José falls to his knees beside Carmen's dead body and cries out, "You can arrest me. I killed her. Oh, Carmen, my Carmen." And the opera comes to an end.

Wolfgang Amadeus Mozart (1756–1791)

2
THE COMPOSER

Add Some Music

Because of its abstract quality, music can strike closer to the heart of human emotions and experiences than anything else man has invented. Through music, a composer can penetrate below the surface and stir feelings of love, jealousy, homesickness, devotion, and more.

For example, the composer can, without words, create a character through the use of a melody alone. It may be a simple tune, almost a ditty, as in *Die Zauberflöte* (*The Magic Flute*). When Papageno, the naive bird-catcher, introduces himself, Mozart uses the simplest means to characterize this gentle, comic man. In *Tosca*, the very essence of evil is suggested by Giacomo Puccini when he introduces the villainous police chief, Scarpia, with ponderous chords, dark and ominous, played *fortissimo* by the orchestra. The presence of mental illness is suggested by Alban Berg in *Wozzeck* through the use of unstable harmonies that have an anguished sound.

In his mammoth four-part work, *Der Ring des Nibelungen (The Ring of the Nibelungs)*, Richard Wagner uses particular bits of melody, harmony, rhythm, or orchestral color to announce each character whenever he or she appears, either onstage or in the minds or conversations of other characters. This "announcement" is called a *leitmotiv*, and it assists the audience in keeping track of a complicated plot line.

Although he carried it further than any other opera composer, Wagner didn't originate this leitmotiv method. There are countless examples in works for the musical stage from Mozart's *Idomeneo* to Ruggiero Leoncavallo's *I Pagliacci (The Clowns)*. Even in modern American musicals, leitmotiv figures strongly in Meredith Willson's *The Music Man*, Leonard Bernstein's *Candide*, and Stephen Sondheim's *Sweeney Todd*.

A skillful composer can create a bit of magic that is impossible for a writer: the expression of several points of view at the same time. This simultaneous expression may be heard in a duet, quartet, sextet, or in a large singing choral ensemble. In the quartet from *Rigoletto*, Verdi and his librettist, Piave, have outlined a key scene which places two sets of leading characters on either side of a high wall so that they are not seen by each other, though the audience is able to see both pairs at the same time. Each character has a single piece of information to relate, yet through skillful compositional technique, their four "messages" are blended into a unified and melodic quartet. On one side of the wall, the playboy Duke of Mantua requests a love tryst with the flirtatious Maddalena, while she keeps putting him off with insincere laughter and ridicule. On the other side of the wall, the unhappy heroine, Gilda, sings of the duke's infidelity, while her father, Rigoletto, tells her of his promise to take revenge on the fickle duke. The four characters express

Gioacchino Rossini (1792–1868) composer of *The Barber of Seville*

themselves simultaneously, each with his or her own characteristic melody. Yet Verdi manages to combine their individual messages into one glorious quartet. What would have taken four times as long to relate in words alone is shortened, yet heightened, with music.

A composer can also comment on the words of the text. Modest Mussorgsky uses musical tricks to illustrate the complexity of a dramatic situation in the tavern scene of *Boris Godunov*. When the fugitive Gregori must escape from the Russian police by an unfamiliar route leading to freedom and the Lithuanian border, Mussorgsky underlines the roundaboutness of the di-

63

rections for escape given to Gregori by the innkeeper. In the accompaniment, he introduces a circle of musical key signatures. Each time a different road or landmark is mentioned, a new key signature appears, six within the space of nine musical measures. Mussorgsky starts with B major, goes to D-sharp minor, then to E major, F-sharp major, B major, G-sharp minor, G-sharp major, E-sharp major, and then lands back at B major, which is like home base, indicating the arrival of the traveler, Gregori, at the road leading to Lithuania and safety.

With this kind of detective work, a careful and imaginative listener can discover all kinds of musical jokes. In the first act of *Der Rosenkavalier*, the princess holds court for a succession of daily visitors who seek her favor. Among the many gift bearers is an animal vendor who tries to present her with the gift of a small poodle. He insists that the dog is a perfect pet, and completely housebroken. Yet in the orchestral accompaniment, Richard Strauss cleverly denies that fact with a light descending staccato scale of watery notes in a high register. The dynamic level is indicated in the score as *pianissimo* (*pp*).

In *The Marriage of Figaro*, one discovers Mozart's feeling about the eighteenth-century concept of a man forced to wear animal horns on his head because he has been made a cuckold by an unfaithful wife. In the last-act aria, "Aprite un po" ("If men would look about them"), when Figaro hints at the possible infidelity of his own wife, Susanna, and at his fear of being cuckolded, the French *horns* in the orchestra introduce a hunting horn phrase, clearly a hint of the ultimate disgrace and a subtle joke for the audience.

Most operas are preceded by an *overture*: a short composition for the orchestra alone. In the early days, Christoph Willibald Gluck and Mozart wrote overtures to set the mood of the work and to settle down the talkers and latecomers before the curtain rose. In later years, Gioacchino Rossini, Verdi, Gounod, and others included melodies from the arias in their overtures.

By the turn of the century, Puccini and Richard Strauss did away with lengthy overtures. In most of their works, the orchestra plays only a few bars, the curtain goes up, and the action begins.

As overtures changed style, so did the size of the orchestra. In the eighteenth century, Mozart's orchestra contained about fifty players; in the nineteenth century, Verdi's grew to eighty; later, Wagner and Richard Strauss composed for orchestras of over one hundred instrumentalists.

Operas that are composed throughout—in other words, where music accompanies all the words: arias, ensembles, and the transitional material called recitatives—are known as grand operas. Most of the works heard in large opera houses today are in this category. Works that include spoken dialogue without musical accompaniment are known by such other names as singspiels (The Magic Flute), comic operas (H.M.S. Pinafore), operetta (The Merry Widow), or musical comedy (Guys and Dolls).

There are in fact two separate opera houses in Paris—the Opéra, where grand operas are performed, and the Opéra-Comique, where those works with spoken dialogue are played. There are similar separations in Vienna—the State Opera House and the Volkstheater—and in other major European cities as well. In New York, the Metropolitan concentrates for the most part on grand opera productions, while Broadway theaters are the realm of musicals with spoken dialogue. Recently, however, the Met and the New York City Opera have begun to include works by Kurt Weill, George Gershwin, and Victor Herbert—works with spoken dialogue. The borderline is never clear. Broadway theaters have presented The Saint of Bleecker Street by Gian Carlo Menotti, Regina by Marc Blitzstein, and The Rape of Lucretia by Benjamin Britten, all composed in varying grand opera styles.

A scene from Mozart's *Così fan Tutte*, his comic opera of lovers in disguise and romantic mix-ups. An Indiana University production.

Regardless of the type of opera, the compositions most remembered by audiences are the *arias.* These individual songs, which express inner feelings of love or fear or some other emotional state of a character, are the melodies whistled and hummed long after the performance is over. Many arias become hit tunes.

The *recitative,* on the other hand, is the connecting material between arias and ensembles, where general interplay between characters is expressed. These segments further the plot and help to differentiate the characters. They are delivered in the rhythm and tempo of speech, but are uttered in musical tones. It is this "talk" that moves the story along. The *recitativo secco* (secco means "dry" in Italian) was used in early seventeenth-century operas and through Mozart's time with the singing line accompanied by a single-keyboard or simple-stringed instrument marking only essential chords and sparse harmonies. *Recitativo accompagnato* (accompanied recitative) originated in the late eighteenth century after Mozart and was written and played with the same texture and orchestration as the rest of the opera.

A scene from Verdi's last opera, *Falstaff,* written in his eightieth year and based on Shakespeare's *The Merry Wives of Windsor.*

Many of today's most popular operas are skillful blends of recitative and aria, and it is difficult to tell where one form leaves off and the other takes over. Wagner rebelled against the aria/recitative form by writing works of seamless texture and unending melody. Claude Debussy in *Pelléas et Mélisande,* and Berg in *Wozzeck,* created works of such continuous interweaving that no set arias are distinguishable.

In seventeenth-century France, dancing superseded singing, making ballet an integral part of every operatic performance. Called *tragédies-lyriques,* these operas were the grandest of the grand spectacles. Jean-Baptiste Lully and Jean-Philippe Rameau were the preeminent composers of this form. Louis XIV, the Sun King, ordered these lavish spectacles to be staged for his court entertainments. In fact, the king himself danced in some of his royal diversions.

Subsequently, dance continued to be included in French grand opera for two centuries. There are long sections of music for ballet in Gounod's *Faust,* and in Camille Saint-Saëns's *Samson et Dalila.* Even Bizet's *Carmen* had to answer the demand for dance. In the first Viennese production, a long ballet outside

Richard Wagner (1813–1883)

RIGHT
Giuseppe Verdi (1813–1901)

FAR RIGHT
Giacomo Puccini (1858–1924)

the bullring was interpolated within Act IV, using music from the composer's *L'Arlésienne* suite. This tradition continues today.

Although dance added spectacle and grandeur to opera and also offered relief from the more static singing elements, some composers disregarded the ballet, believing that it interrupted the flow of their work. Throughout the nineteenth century, however, it was unthinkable to produce an opera in Paris without a ballet. The audience expected it. When Wagner first presented *Tannhäuser* in Paris sixteen years after its Dresden premiere, he had to write a whole new scene, set in the court of Venus, which consisted of pagan rites danced to voluptuous music.

Italian composers also made use of ballet. In its third act, Ponchielli's *La Gioconda* has an almost full-length ballet, "The Dance of the Hours." Verdi's *Aida* has a variety of dances in the "Triumphal Scene" in Act II. In other countries, dance was important to Bedřich Smetana's *Prodaná Nevěsta (The Bartered Bride)*, Alexander Borodin's *Prince Igor*, and Johann Strauss' *Die Fledermaus (The Bat)*.

In American musical theater, dancing became fully inte-

grated with the storyline. Rodgers and Hart's *On Your Toes* introduced a lengthy ballet called "Slaughter on Tenth Avenue." The dances in Rodgers and Hammerstein's *Oklahoma!* moved the plot forward inventively. Leonard Bernstein's *West Side Story* had choreographed street rumbles, gymnasium dances, and dream ballet sequences, necessary elements to the story.

Composers of operas, like composers of symphonies, concerti, and chamber music, fit generally into one of four major styles. The seventeenth century, when opera began, was the *Baroque* period, with such composers as Francesco Cavalli, Henry Purcell, Monteverdi, and Lully. Music of this era was characterized by pomp and splendor, a feeling of extravagance. It was a period of ornamentation and improvisation.

Eighteenth-century music—often called *Classical*—is basically formal and balanced with a sense of stability and tradition that is said to be intellectual. Mozart, Gluck, George Frederick Handel, and Franz Joseph Haydn were composers in this period.

The *Romantic* era spans most of the nineteenth century, when music was highly emotional and subjective, allowing great freedom of form. Peter Ilyich Tchaikovsky, Wagner, Verdi, and Puccini are numbered among the Romantic composers.

Twentieth-century music, loosely called the period of *Modern* music, comprises various styles, among them impressionist, expressionist, atonal, serial, neoclassic, and aleatory. Modern composers include Richard Strauss, Debussy, Gershwin, and Britten.

Whatever the style or period in which it was written, all Western music uses the same basic twelve tones of the chromatic scale for its melodies and harmonies, the same time-signatures and note values for its rhythms, and, with few exceptions, the same orchestral instruments and human voices for its colors. They are the tools of the opera composer's craft, and he uses them imaginatively and skillfully to create moods and tell stories that entertain and move audiences as no other expression can.

The first-act from *Madama Butterfly*, based on David Belasco's play, in which Cio-Cio-San (Butterfly) is cursed by her uncle, a Japanese priest, for renouncing her traditional religion by marrying the American naval officer, B. F. Pinkerton.

THE COMPOSER OF CARMEN

Although the composer of *Carmen* had written twenty-seven operas by the time he was thirty-four, only four had been published. *Carmen*, his last, was to become his masterpiece. It is the single work that has guaranteed his inclusion on the list of the world's most recognized composers.

Alexandre César Léopold Bizet (called Georges) was born into a musical family in Paris. His father was a teacher of voice, specializing in coaching opera singers. An uncle, his mother's brother, was a well-known singer who appeared in concerts in the French courts.

As a child, young Georges was encouraged by his parents to become a musician. There was no social stigma attached to the life-style of a musician in those days, and Georges was a fine pianist, with perfect pitch and a spectacular knowledge of harmony. At age nine, even though it was against the rules to admit anyone so young, he was enrolled at the Paris Conservatoire, where he won many prizes for his compositions. His early orchestral work, *Symphony in C*, written in 1855 when he was seventeen, was not discovered until the 1930s and is played today throughout the world on concert programs and as the score for the well-known ballet.

At nineteen, Bizet won the Prix de Rome, one of the most prestigious prizes in music, which allowed him three years' study in Rome while living in the luxurious Villa Medici. (A large sum of money was also part of the award.) Bizet completed several operas there, and on his triumphant return to Paris, he served as orchestrator for other composers and wrote operas on commission for various producing companies.

He married Geneviève Halévy, daughter of his old composition teacher, Jacques Halévy, the well-known composer of the opera *La Juive*, and cousin to Ludovic Halévy, one of the librettists of *Carmen*. When the Franco-Prussian War was declared, Bizet served in the French army, but saw no action.

Bizet received the commission to write *Carmen* in 1872, but he did not complete it until two years later, and it was not produced until March 1875. Due to financial problems of the Paris Opéra-Comique, it looked for a while as if it would not be produced at all. In the interim Bizet was forced to work on other projects, among them the composition of incidental music for Alphonse Daudet's play *L'Arlésienne* and the full-length opera *Don Rodrigue*, which was never completed.

Since composing is an occupation with an unreliable income, Bizet gave hundreds of piano lessons to young people at twenty francs for half an hour. A hundred years ago, twenty francs was about four dollars. Living with his constantly ailing wife, their sickly child, and a neurotic mother-in-law did not make things easy for him.

ABOVE Georges Bizet (1838–1875) in a photograph taken when he was thirty-five, about the time he was writing *Carmen.*

ABOVE, RIGHT A portrait of the twenty-two-year-old Bizet by his friend Félix-Henri Giacomotti, who described his subject as "the very embodiment of adolescent genius."

RIGHT A sketch by G. Planté of Bizet when he returned to Paris from his years in Italy as the recipient of the Prix de Rome.

His opera *Carmen* is set in Seville and is as Spanish as one can imagine. Yet Bizet never set foot on Spanish soil. The locales of some of his other operas are also exotic: *Djamileh* is set in Egypt (where he never went); *Les Pêcheurs de Perles (The Pearl Fishers)* takes place in Ceylon, and certainly he had not traveled that far from France. He researched the music of Spain, however, in preparation for writing *Carmen*, and there still exists a library slip from the Paris Conservatory on which he requested information about Spanish folk songs. He chose one melody that he used almost note for note as his "Habanera." The "folk" tune "El Arreglito" was actually composed by the Spaniard Sebastián Yradier. In his typically conscientious way, Bizet acknowledged Yradier in the published score.

Bizet's nomination to the Legion of Honor, the highest award France gives to its distinguished citizens and artists, was announced on the morning of the world premiere of *Carmen* at the Opéra-Comique. That night, after the badly received performance, one member of the scandalized audience was heard to say, "They announced it this morning because they knew that by tonight it would no longer be possible to give him a decoration."

After its premiere, *Carmen* was recommended for production in Vienna, but only on condition that the spoken words be sung to fully composed accompaniments (recitatives). The contract with the Vienna Opera House was finally settled one day before Bizet's death, so he was never able to compose the recitatives. They were written by his friend, Ernest Guiraud, an American composer who was born in New Orleans and are a remarkable example of one composer adapting himself to another composer's style. It is the Bizet-Guiraud version of *Carmen* that one hears most often today.

PART TWO

THE
INTERPRETERS

Jenny Lind (1820–1887), "the Swedish Nightingale," in a drawing framed by Mr. Genin, a New York hatter, to commemorate his purchase of the first ticket sold for her American debut concert. The price, in 1850, was $225.

3
THE SINGER

Give Us a Star

Everyone goes to see and hear the star—on the screen, on the stage, and especially in the opera house.

No box office suffers when Luciano Pavarotti, Placido Domingo, Leontyne Price, or Joan Sutherland appears. In former years, there were Rosa Ponselle, Leonard Warren, Lotte Lehmann, Beniamino Gigli and, more recently, Maria Callas. Opera stars have invaded the movie theaters, too—Geraldine Farrar, Grace Moore, Lily Pons, Risë Stevens, and Ezio Pinza. It is the same in opera as on Broadway, where stars like Ethel Merman, Mary Martin, and Lena Horne insure sold-out houses for long-run musicals.

A name from the past that is synonymous with great singing, glamour, and international appeal is Jenny Lind, "the Swedish

Nightingale.'' She became a star in European opera houses in the nineteenth century, and music was written especially for her by Giacomo Meyerbeer and Verdi. Her portrayal of Donizetti and Bellini heroines became legend. She appeared on the stage when she was thirteen years old and sang her first operatic role when she was fifteen. The possessor of an extraordinarily wide vocal range (see Vocal Range Chart, page 98), she was unsurpassed at pyrotechnics. Yet her interpretation of humble ballads was simplicity itself.

In 1850 Jenny Lind was booked by the master American showman and circus impresario, P. T. Barnum, to tour the United States. For two years, she was the sensation of the American continent and earned enormous sums of money, much of which she donated to her favorite charities. There probably has never been a singer before or since who was so greatly acclaimed.

More recently, Maria Jeritza of the Metropolitan Opera was called ''a genuine twenty-four-carat prima donna of the old school.'' She belonged to the period of opera known as the ''Golden Age,'' a span of two decades at the beginning of the twentieth century. It was a time for many glorious opera singers—Enrico Caruso, Jean and Edouard De Reszke, Emmy Destinn, Marcel Journet, and Antonio Scotti—and it was a time when opera singers were accorded the mass adulation given today to rock singers and superstar athletes.

Maria Jeritza was a tall, imperious woman with an exquisite face and shimmering blonde hair. She was married three times, and rumors of her close relationships with European royalty added spice to her already glamorous life. Once, when speaking of her vast collection of jewels, she sniffed scornfully about current prima donnas and said, ''Flowers! If they had tried to give me only flowers, I would have laughed in their faces.'' Jeritza created roles in operas by Erich Korngold, Leoš Janáček, and in two operas by Richard Strauss, *Ariadne auf*

Maria Jeritza (1887–1982), the Czechoslovakian soprano who made
her Metropolitan Opera debut in 1921 as Marietta in Erich Korngold's
Die Tote Stadt and was celebrated for her interpretation of *Tosca*.

Enrico Caruso (1873–1921),
the Italian tenor who made his American
debut with the Metropolitan Opera in 1903
as the Duke in Verdi's *Rigoletto*. Some say
he possessed the greatest singing voice
ever heard.

Naxos and *Die Frau ohne Schatten.* She died in New Jersey in 1982 at the age of ninety-four.

The Italian-born Enrico Caruso was *the* star and chief attraction of the Metropolitan Opera Company for almost twenty years. His glorious tenor voice aided by his fantastic breath control, which gave him the ability to spin out incredibly long phrases with ease, was heard in all the Italian and French repertories. He came before the public at a propitious time—at the beginning of the budding phonograph-recording industry. His reputation to this day is confirmed by the rare originals and reprints of over two hundred recordings.

Caruso was both a romantic lead and a fine comedian. His famous vocal effect, a gasp of passion, was referred to as "the Caruso sob," a rough attack on a note used to accent his fervor. To emphasize a phrase, Caruso occasionally delayed the beat, the same trick that later made Ethel Merman one of Broadway's greatest pop singers. When asked the requisites for a great singer, Caruso said, "A big chest, a big mouth, ninety percent memory, ten percent intelligence, lots of hard work, and something in the heart." So great was his passion for singing that he sang through a throat hemorrhage in a performance of Gaetano Donizetti's *L'Elisir d'Amore* (*The Elixir of Love*) at the Brooklyn Academy of Music the year before he died. Even sixty years after his death, his remarkable voice is the model for all great contemporary tenors.

Feodor Chaliapin was a Russian-born bass who appeared at the Metropolitan Opera well into the twentieth century. A handsome man with a superb physique, he spent most of his free evenings attending theater performances to observe acting techniques. He also spent time in art museums and with painters, which helped him become a master of characterization and stage makeup. His major triumph was the title role of Mussorgsky's *Boris Godunov*. It is said that his genius as an actor would by itself have gained him fame, and that his gestures illuminated the very structure and essence of the music. Chaliapin excelled in the "devil" roles in *Faust* and *Mefistofele*, as well as in the comic bass roles by Rossini, Donizetti, and Mozart.

Stars dazzle the public. They provide the glamour sometimes missing from our lives. And they are immortalized by such commonplace things as famous foods served in restaurants or at home. Chicken Tetrazzini, for example—a combination of chicken breast, macaroni, and mushrooms, baked in a wine, cream, and cheese sauce—was named after Luisa Tetrazzini, an Italian coloratura soprano who made the role of Violetta in *La*

Luisa Tetrazzini (1871–1940), the Italian coloratura soprano who made her American debut in 1908 singing Violetta in Verdi's *La Traviata* at Hammerstein's Manhattan Opera House.

RIGHT
Feodor Chaliapin (1873–1938), the Russian bass who made his Metropolitan Opera debut in 1907 as Mefistofele in Boito's opera. He played the title role in a film version of *Don Quixote*.

Traviata famous at the Metropolitan Opera House. Spaghetti à la Caruso, pasta served with a sauce of chicken livers and tomatoes, was a favorite with Enrico Caruso. Pêche Melba, a rich and tasty dessert consisting of half a peach served with vanilla ice cream and a clear raspberry sauce, was named after the Australian coloratura soprano, Dame Nellie Melba. She was also immortalized by *another* comestible—although not so rich or

Nellie Melba (1861–1931), the Australian coloratura soprano who made her American debut in 1893 in Donizetti's *Lucia di Lammermoor* at the Metropolitan Opera House. Saint-Saëns wrote the opera *Hélène* for her.

tasty—Melba toast, a crisp, thinly sliced, toasted bread, usually served with a combination of hors d'oeuvres at cocktail parties or eaten by people who are dieting.

While the poet's words and the composer's music are the center of the creation of an operatic work, it is the singer who receives most of the adulation in the form of applause and approval at each performance. And rightly so, for it is through the singers that the ideas of the composer and the librettist come to life.

Rossini said that "a good singer should be nothing but an able interpreter of the ideas of the master, the composer." And Wagner wrote, "The oldest, truest, most beautiful organ of music, the origin to which alone our music owes its being, is the human voice." Robert Merrill, a Metropolitan Opera baritone, merely said, "When in doubt, sing loud!"

The leading female singer in opera is sometimes called a diva. This term comes from the Latin word for goddess. Even if she doesn't quite reach divine status, the female lead is nonetheless at least referred to as a prima donna, Italian for "first lady."

In the history of opera, there was one tradition for singers that is considered absurd today. In the seventeenth and eighteenth centuries, many male singers submitted to physical tampering to keep their voice ranges in unnaturally high registers similar to those of boy sopranos. This enabled them to play female roles. Known as castrati, these adult men had both the experience and the musicianship to display great vocal skill and brilliance. Today these operatic roles are transposed to lower registers for men or given to women. Earlier, however, women were not allowed to appear on stage since acting was considered a wicked profession.

In the eighteenth and nineteenth centuries, many male character roles were written in the woman's vocal range with the intention that women should sing them. These impersonations are known as *pants roles* because the character would wear a costume of doublet and breeches. Among the most famous still performed today are Cherubino in Mozart's *The Marriage of Figaro*, Octavian in Richard Strauss' *Der Rosenkavalier*, and Hänsel in Engelbert Humperdinck's *Hänsel und Gretel*. These impersonations are sometimes confusing on stage, but the sound of contrasting women's voices blending together provides a haunting beauty found in no other combination. The finale of Strauss' *Der Rosenkavalier*, for example, a trio for two sopranos and a mezzo (a pants role), is one of the auditory glories in all opera. The similarity of range and the subtle differences of tone color create sounds that are exquisite. Even in non-pants roles, the sound of two or more women's voices in harmony can be spine-tingling, as in the "Flower Duet" from Puccini's *Madama Butterfly*, the trio of Auntie and her two nieces in Britten's *Peter Grimes*, or the duet of the two priestesses in Vincenzo Bellini's *Norma*.

To recreate and interpret the music is the role of the singer—surely an art in itself. Many interpretive artists claim that when they perform, they try to think of themselves as the composers of the music so that they can get closer to the real interpretation.

There is a seldom-used treatise, the Rutz theory of interpretation, that holds a key for all interpreters of music. Josef Rutz, a nineteenth-century German musician who lived in Munich, taught his own technique of singing. He advocated the use of different positions of the singer's torso muscles in relation to the song being interpreted.

Rutz stressed that in order to properly interpret a composer's music it was necessary to study the physiology of that composer. The pianist must sit in the same position as the composer must have sat at the keyboard. Mozart, for example, was a slight figure who sat rather upright—as opposed to Johannes Brahms, who was a rather heavy man and probably slouched. Brahms's large stomach obviously kept him a good distance from his piano keys. Rutz states that only in this physically imitative way can the interpretive artist recreate the real flavor of the music. He prescribed this method for singers as well as for instrumentalists. The contemporary master of opera production, Boris Goldovsky, has used the Rutz method successfully with his student singers. (I have been present at his demonstrations of the "composer as pianist" technique, and the results are eye-openers.)

A few years ago at a piano recital in Newport, Rhode Island, I witnessed the American debut of a young Russian whose concert contained the works of Alexander Scriabin, a Russian composer of great piano music. The young man, Andrei Gavrilov, played a Scriabin sonata in such an authoritative manner that I felt I was in the presence of the composer and that Gavrilov was improvising the composition as he went along. It was a thrilling musical experience that came from the pianist's intuition about, and kinship with, the composer. This improvisatory quality is the test of a truly great interpreter. It can be observed in Leonard Bernstein's orchestral concerts, especially when he conducts the works of Mahler and Tchaikovsky.

Sometimes the greatest interpreters in opera are those singers whose roles were written especially for them. In our own time, Britten wrote most of the leading tenor roles in his operas—from the early Peter Grimes to his last stage work, Death in Venice—for his close friend, Peter Pears. Menotti has written roles for Marie Powers and for Beverly Sills; Samuel Barber created Antony and Cleopatra for Leontyne Price. Bellini composed Norma and La Sonnambula (The Sleepwalker) for Giuditta Pasta; Rossini made alterations in The Barber of Seville for Adelina Patti.

Other composers have hoped for perfect combinations of acting and singing in one artist so that their operas would come alive. Two outstanding examples of singers who filled their most famous roles to the delight of their composers were the

Scottish soprano Mary Garden, and the Italian baritone Victor Maurel. Garden was the first to sing the role of Mélisande, and she was coached by the composer, Claude Debussy. Through her superb acting, she became the shadowy illusion, the fragile marionette of the playwright's conception. In Verdi's *Otello*, Maurel created the role of the villain, Iago. Considered the foremost dramatic artist of his time, he was also chosen to impersonate the blustery main character Sir John of Verdi's last opera, *Falstaff*; he pleased the composer and created a sensation at the premiere.

Because of their rare vocal and histrionic abilities, many singers have been largely responsible for restoring long-forgotten works to the stage. The late Maria Callas' dramatic talent had much to do with the success of the modern revivals of Luigi Cherubini's *Médée* (*Medea*) and Bellini's *La Sonnambula*. Callas always sought the heart of the drama in the music, expressing it intuitively and completely. She would often sacrifice the beauty of tone if it did not express the core of the dramatic situation.

Another contemporary soprano, Beverly Sills, recreated the famous English queens, the title roles in Donizetti's *Anna Bolena* and *Maria Stuarda*. Sills' vocal abilities include agile and accurate coloratura, and she possesses an intuitive feeling for impersonating the regal yet sympathetic qualities of these doomed women.

Mary Garden (1877–1967), the Scottish soprano who created the role of Mélisande in Debussy's *Pelléas et Mélisande*. Her operatic debut was made under dramatic circumstances when she replaced the ailing prima donna during a performance of Charpentier's *Louise* at the Paris Opéra-Comique. She became the head of the Chicago Opera Company in 1921, and in that year their losses exceeded one million dollars.

Claudia Muzio (1889–1936), the Italian soprano who made her first American appearance as Tosca at the Metropolitan Opera House in 1916. She was a leading member of the Chicago Opera Company for eleven years.

Claudia Muzio's Violetta in Verdi's *La Traviata* has served as the definitive interpretation of that role, which she sang with the Chicago Opera Company in the 1920s. The early recordings of her reading of the fateful letter in the last act acclaim her artistry. Her diction is so pure that each vowel sound undergoes subtle changes to project the character's emotional anguish.

Other singers added touches of characterization and bits of stage business that have made their interpretations memorable. The soprano Maria Jeritza created a sensation at the Metropolitan Opera House sixty years ago when she sang the title role in Puccini's *Tosca*. In the second act, when she struggled and

Victor Maurel (1848–1923), the French baritone who created leading roles in Verdi's *Otello* and *Falstaff,* here seen as Mozart's *Don Giovanni.* He was well known as an actor on the French stage. He studied painting and also became a stage designer. He retired in New York City as a teacher of voice.

pleaded with Scarpia, the head of the Roman secret police, to save her lover from the firing squad, she was accidentally thrown to the floor. Without thinking, she sang the famous aria "Vissi d'arte" ("I lived for art") from that position. It became the most talked-about staging of the season, and many directors and sopranos have incorporated it into their performances ever since.

Great opera singers are worthy of public acclaim. Consider their training and their responsibilities. They must study all facets of music: not only its literature, but also its theory and history. They must learn vocal production and breath control.

They must learn many languages, master good diction, know stage deportment, and acquire acting techniques. They must learn how to create character makeup. They must be able to memorize lengthy musical scores and texts. They must maintain hearty constitutions to sustain themselves through daily work that is physically and mentally strenuous. The amount of energy expended in the performance of many operatic roles is equal to that expended by an athlete in the Olympics.

Some years ago, while rehearsing the staging of Menotti's *The Medium* with the leading singers, I found that it was more convenient to use my living room rather than the rented rehearsal studio. A pianist accompanied Lyuba Senderovna, who played Madame Flora, the phony spiritualist. Senderovna needed coaching in the intricate movements of the confrontation scene with her young assistant Toby, whose role called for him to aid in her sham séances. In the scene we rehearsed that afternoon, Senderovna had to beat the boy, actually taking a whip to his bare back—a chilling scene on stage. After running through the action several times, we were interrupted by loud knocks at my apartment door. Several New York policemen burst into the room with guns drawn, ready to break up the furious domestic battle and stop the blood-curdling screams.

Because opera stories are heavily laced with life-or-death situations, revenge and murder, opera singers must know how to produce a variety of such screams. But they must know how to scream and shriek without damaging those two delicate vibrating bands in their throats, the vocal cords. Even when singing soft lyrical passages, they must be heard in every part of a three-thousand-seat auditorium. And they must be heard above a one-hundred-piece orchestra without the benefit, or the distortion, of a microphone. Most Broadway musicals now use amplification systems for practically everyone, but the electronic devil has yet to invade most opera houses, and I hope that it never will.

Creators of the leading roles in the 1947 Broadway production of Gian Carlo Menotti's *The Medium* (from left to right): Leo Coleman as Toby, Marie Powers as Madame Flora, and Evelyn Keller as Monica.

The singer's voice is his most precious equipment, and he studies for years how to protect and improve it. As the great mezzo-soprano Christa Ludwig remarked, "You must be careful with your voice. It's like a raw egg—once it's kaput, it's kaput!" But used wisely, the voice of an opera singer, like that of an actor, can last through a long and fruitful career.

Opera singers, unlike actors on stage or screen, are truly international artists. They travel by plane to every opera house in the world, from La Scala in Milan to the Teatro Colón in Buenos Aires, from Tokyo's Bunka Kaikan to London's Covent Garden, singing roles with different casts, under different conductors, in different stage settings and costumes.

In Frankfurt there might be a series of steep ramps in the first act of *Carmen*. In Paris the same scene might be designed with a flight of steps. In Rome the steps might be on the opposite side of the stage. And in New York, still a different layout. With little rehearsal, and sometimes without even being introduced to the leading man, Carmen must flirt and interact with Don José, adjust her vocal level to his, and hold her own in the crowd scenes—all within a few hours of getting off the plane, and in front of three thousand spectators. No wonder it has sometimes been said of certain leading divas, "They just stand in the middle of the stage and sing!" Perhaps that's all they have the strength to do.

Today singers are trying to allow themselves more rehearsal time for both old and new productions. Opera house managements are cooperating by booking casts into a block of time, allowing for a number of performances of the same operas with the same casts. Opera is similar to true repertory theater, where the same casts appear in several alternating productions.

Along with a more enlightened management and public, singers are becoming increasingly aware of the importance of the quality of acting and of presenting convincing characterizations. They no longer try to get by with only a beautiful sound or turn of phrase. The acting skills that Maria Callas developed for her portrayal of Violetta in *La Traviata* or Norma in Bellini's opera are on a par with the techniques of many Oscar, Emmy, and Tony winners in the more popular media. As opera continues to attract a larger public, there will perhaps be a new annual awards ceremony on television, the "Mimi" (named for the

The séance scene from Menotti's *The Medium,* telecast over the NBC network from WPTZ Philadelphia in 1947. From left to right: Emil Markow, Lois Hunt as Monica, Theodora Brandon, Mary Davenport as Madame Flora, and Edith Evans.

heroine of *La Bohème*) for international recognition of the year's outstanding performances.

Now that opera is seen on television by millions of viewers, there is a growing tendency for leading singers to trim their waistlines. Renata Scotto, on seeing herself as Mimi in the 1977 telecast from the Metropolitan, swore she would lose weight and subsequently shed forty-three pounds. "I thank television for that," she said. "You have to make the character believable, and to make the character believable, you have to look right." Televised opera has other production problems. Being an intimate medium, television carries its greatest impact through the use of close-ups. Operatic singing, by nature, is not the most photogenic activity. Singers often strain visibly, present an unattractive display of teeth and larynx, and glue their eyes on the off-camera conductor.

In the early days of televised opera, both the singers and the orchestra performed together "live," sometimes in separate studios, and their results were relayed to one another by loudspeakers and headphones. Later, prerecording of the voices became common practice. Herbert von Karajan, the internationally known maestro—who has produced, staged, and conducted numerous television operas in Europe—goes even further, and prerecords both the singers and the orchestra track, adjusting the mixture in the control room. This requires his singers to lip-sync, a practice that forfeits reality and immediacy. Because the singer does not have to rely on accuracy or strain to imitate himself, he is apt to merely mouth the words, giving little semblance of enacting the role. It's all too polite. Good lip-synchronization is difficult to achieve and sometimes calls for many retakes; the result is often not pleasant to watch. I find this practice abhorrent, so I was elated when I saw some unedited footage from a series of Gilbert and Sullivan operettas recently completed in London. The producers had wisely chosen to prerecord only the orchestra and the large singing-dancing chorus. They insisted that the principals sing live in full voice for camera and microphone, accompanied by the orchestral playback. The results are exciting and believable.

Singers today possess abilities undreamed of by performers of the past. And many of today's artists have acquired additional skills unknown to yesterday's stars. Hildegard Behrens, a leading international dramatic soprano, is a practicing lawyer; Eileen Farrell, one of the most glorious voices ever to sing at the Met, is also an interpreter of jazz songs and blues; Placido Domingo, one of the most acclaimed romantic tenors in the world today, is an accomplished pianist who once played the rehearsals for Anna Sokolow's modern dance company in Mexico City; Sherrill Milnes, the outstanding American baritone, is studying to become a conductor; and Julia Migenes-Johnson, the young soprano who sang the title role in Alban Berg's *Lulu* in a recent Met telecast, began her career as a dancer.

VOCAL RANGE CHART

With outstanding contemporary singers in each category

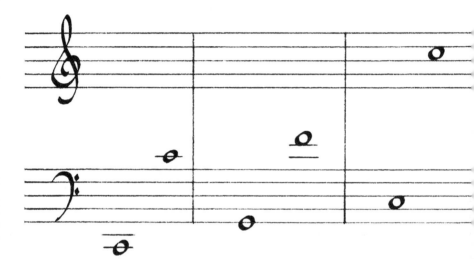

BASS	BARITONE	TENOR
Boris Christoff	Walter Berry	José Carreras
Nicolai Ghiaurov	D. Fischer-Dieskau	Placido Domingo
Kurt Moll	Hakan Hagegard	Nicolai Gedda
Samuel Ramey	Sherrill Milnes	Alfredo Kraus
Martti Talvela	Hermann Prey	Luciano Pavarotti
José van Dam	Bernd Weikl	Jon Vickers

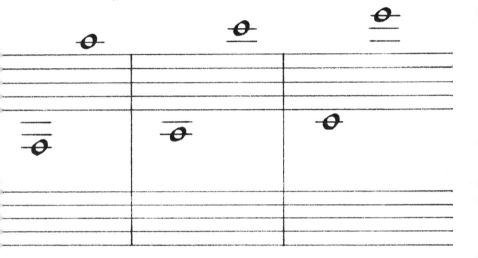

MEZZO-SOPRANO & CONTRALTO	SOPRANO	COLORATURA SOPRANO
Teresa Berganza	Montserrat Caballé	Edita Gruberova
Maureen Forrester	Birgit Nilsson	Roberta Peters
Marilyn Horne	Leontyne Price	Lucia Popp
Christa Ludwig	Renata Scotto	Beverly Sills
Yvonne Minton	Teresa Stratas	Joan Sutherland
Frederica von Stade	Kiri Te Kanawa	Ruth Welting

Célestine Galli-Marié
(1840–1905),
who created the role of Carmen
at the 1875 premiere.

THE EARLIEST CARMEN

The role of Carmen, one of the most difficult to perform in the entire operatic repertory, is also one of the most sought-after roles. Although Carmen does not make her entrance until halfway through the first act, she is on stage for most of the remaining acts and sings much of that time. Vocally it is a strenuous role, and it calls for a variety of acting skills as well. The performance is apt to fall flat without a remarkable singing actress, who must appear slim, attractive, and skilled as a dancer. Who could possibly measure up to these demands? When the opera was merely an idea in the minds of Bizet and his librettists, the first singer suggested for the role was Zulma Bouffar, a charming leading lady who began her career singing risqué French songs in cafés and graduated to leading roles in

Offenbach operettas. But it was rumored that Bouffar did not wish to play a part in which she was stabbed to death. Then Marie Rôze, a very proper and successful singer, was approached to create the role, but the soprano wrote to Bizet after their interview: ". . . because of the very *scabrous* side of the character . . . the role would not suit me, or more accurately, I would not be suited to it."

The role was then offered to Parisian-born Célestine Galli-Marié, a mezzo-soprano with the dark-skinned aura of a Spanish gypsy. A critic wrote, "She is small and graceful, moves like a cat, has an impish, pert face, and her whole personality seems unruly and mischievous." Galli-Marié turned out to be the perfect Carmen, yet she frequently came late to rehearsals, even missed some, was difficult with her financial demands during contractual arrangements, and wanted changes in the libretto and the music. Bizet rewrote the "Habanera" thirteen times before it satisfied her. (Victor Lhérie, the tenor who created the role of Don José, also asked for changes in some parts of his duets.) The librettists tried to persuade Galli-Marié to subdue her acting, which they thought overdone and vulgar, but she insisted on playing the role as she felt it, and her performance contributed immeasurably to the opera's success.

Over the months of rehearsal, Galli-Marié and Bizet became close friends. For the thirty-first performance, she arrived at the Opéra-Comique in tears and, according to her diary, "in a state of indescribable hyperexcitement." She got through the first two acts, but in the third act, when Carmen foresees her own death in the "Card Trio," a dreadful feeling came over her and she collapsed at the end of the act. Backstage she said, "Nothing is the matter with me, but something dreadful is happening elsewhere." She completed the opera, but the next day, when she heard that Bizet had died the night before, she was unable to sing and the performance was canceled.

The first American to portray Carmen was an eccentric celeb-

Conchita Supervia (1899–1936) in the role of Carmen, which she first sang at age 15 in Italy.

rity who sang the role over five hundred times in many languages. Her name was Minnie Hauk, and she herself had started a rumor that she was not really American, but Spanish, that she had been a female bullfighter before turning to opera, and that her real name was Manuelita Cuchares, ''Queen of the Espadas.'' Nonetheless, she was said to be a great Carmen.

Clara Kellogg claimed that she, not Hauk, was the first Amer-

Emma Calvé
(as Carmen)

ican Carmen, but research shows that her production opened in Philadelphia two days after Minnie Hauk's premiere in New York.

The Carmen thought by many to be the greatest was Emma Calvé, who first introduced authentic gypsy dancing as part of her performance. Her passion was described by a critic as "unbridled." She also had a sense of humor; once she popped a flower into her tenor's mouth just as he was about to begin his big aria, the "Flower Song."

Geraldine Farrar of the Metropolitan Opera was a beauty and the first soprano slim enough to look the way Carmen should. She also starred in Cecil B. De Mille's version of the opera in 1915, ironically a *silent* film.

Another notable and remarkable Carmen was the Spanish mezzo-soprano, Conchita Supervia, who can still be heard on rare recordings. She possessed an incredible vocal range with

unique *chest tones* that would have made your hair stand on end.

Rosa Ponselle, the late great dramatic soprano, undertook the role only a few times at the Metropolitan. The critics panned her portrayal, but copies of a screen test she made for Hollywood certainly contradict their opinions. Her "Habanera" and "Seguidilla" on film are sparkling and vivacious.

Mary Garden played Carmen as a femme fatale and instead of tossing a flower to José at their first meeting, she actually crushed it in his face.

Bruna Castagna was an Italian contralto who sang at the Metropolitan in the 1930s and '40s. She was a very large woman and certainly not the right physical type for Carmen, yet she immersed herself so thoroughly in the role that her own physique seemed to disappear. In both singing and acting, she was the most exciting gypsy I have ever seen.

Backstage of the Opera House in West Berlin.

4
THE STAGE DIRECTOR

Don't Stand There—Do Something!

There is a story of a famous but fussy stage actress who overdid every piece of business. She constantly twisted a handkerchief or bit at her fingernails while enacting a role. The director, in an effort to tone down her activities, shouted "Don't *do* something—just stand there!"

The reverse, however, could be said of some opera singers today, who seem unable to differentiate between the concert platform and the operatic stage. Acting is seemingly beyond them—or was overlooked in their professional training.

Sometimes it's best to minimize. To avoid any action whatsoever during the "Nile Scene" in *Aida* can be particularly satisfying and communicative. In this scene, the Ethiopian princess Aida, disguised as an Egyptian slave girl, resigns herself never to see her country again. Some Aidas move all over the stage during the aria, almost as if they were expressing joy at having the entire set to themselves. Yet in this highly dramatic moment, the soprano can be far more effective in conveying her ambivalent feelings by remaining still and self-contained.

I remember Menotti's instructions to the character Monica in his opera *The Medium*. When Monica discovers the lifeless body of her lover, who has been murdered by her own mother, Menotti suggested that Monica should make a contracting movement from the waist, a sort of a dry-heaving motion as a reaction to seeing the dead body. Then she should hesitatingly try to run out of the room to seek help. She should call out, "Help!", inaudibly at first, then repeat the word until she gains full vocal strength after the third or fourth call. The piercing, fully shouted cry would not be heard until after she had left the stage. In performance, the realistic approach had greater impact than an immediate full-throated scream.

It is the realm of the stage director in opera to blend all the small and large actions of his cast into a completed stage picture. It is his job not only to conceive the style of the production, but also to control the traffic patterns of the actors, and the placement of the sets, furniture, and props. He discusses the characterizations of the roles with the singers and suggests the design styles of costumes, makeup, and lighting.

Porgy, a cripple, confesses his love for Bess, to the approval of the residents of Catfish Row in Gershwin's *Porgy and Bess.*

The four bohemians and their companions
celebrate Christmas Eve at a Paris sidewalk café
in the second act of Puccini's *La Bohème*.

Not too many years ago, the stage director of an opera was
called the *régisseur*, which meant the director of the ballet, a
holdover title from French and other European opera house traditions. Usually a retired singer or someone who knew a little
more about acting and stage movement than the performers he
directed, he was solely responsible for trafficking all of the
stage action. Today that function is entrusted to more imagina-

tive and knowledgeable theatrical creators, and opera staging is often on a level equal to the best in the spoken theater.

It is actually the composer and the librettist who set the framework for the stage director's job through words, stage directions, and character descriptions in the text, and through rhythmic patterns, length of phrases, and choices of orchestration in the score. Together these original creators determine the actors' movements within each scene. No matter how brilliant and innovative the ideas of a director may be, any theatrical stroke that contradicts the music should be thrown out.

Boris Goldovsky has said that the stage action of an opera or of any musical theater production is created from the orchestra pit. When the music is boisterous, the action on stage must reflect that energy. When the music is serene, the stage picture must also be serene.

Matching the rise and fall of this energy with stage activity is one of the fundamental creative duties of the director. Each separate scene has "a temperature of excitement." Although composed by its creators, the mood must appear to the audience to be created by the characters on stage. The proper time to achieve this mirroring is in the moment *before* a change occurs in the music. Then the characters on stage seem to initiate the action *and* the activity in the orchestra. For example: It is quiet on stage. All of a sudden there is a loud knock on the door. A split second later, fury and bustle break out in the orchestra, commenting on the interruption and change of activity.

A study of the music in the score may also determine the basic design of the sets for an opera. The music's tempo and the lengths of orchestral passages tell the director precisely how much time his leading characters need to appear on stage or disappear when they exit. These musical clues enable the director to determine if there should be one or two doorways in the castle hall, or one or several ramps leading offstage from the public square.

In *Peter Grimes*, the changing of the sets is aided by Britten's well suited and perfectly timed "Four Sea Interludes." These purely orchestral tone pictures not only sustain the mood of the ongoing drama, but their loud passages also help to cover the sounds of moving the sets behind the closed curtain in preparation for the next scene.

It is fascinating to discover how much a well-written score can reveal about production design. Through study and examination of the text and music, a knowledgeable director can find answers for large patterns of stage movement as well as for small gestures for a single character.

At a recent International Congress of Verdi Studies held on the West Coast, a performance of *La Forza del Destino (The Force of Destiny)* displayed an example of proper and improper stage direction. In one scene, Leonora assures Alvaro that her heart is bursting with joy at the thought of their planned elopement, and her words are accompanied by the stage direction that "she weeps." At the first performance, the audience laughed out loud at the contrast between words (sung in English) and Leonora's obvious facial expressions of grief. Shortly before the second performance, it was suggested that she weep *exactly* when the instruction appears in the score, at the *first* note of the phrase, instead of afterward. She did, and the spectators did not laugh. They were moved.

In the first scene of Mozart's *The Marriage of Figaro*, Susanna begs her husband-to-be to look at her and admire the new hat she's trying on in front of the mirror at her dressing table. Figaro, however, is too concerned with measuring the room for the placement of new furniture. After repeated entreaties, he finally looks at her. The question is, on which of her ten bids for attention should Figaro put down his tape measure and look at Susanna? Mozart supplies the answer not in the Da Ponte text, but in the music itself—in the melodic line of musical notes. On Susanna's sixth entreaty, a *diminished fifth* (D to A-flat) ap-

Papageno, a bird-catcher, confesses his happiness to
Pamina, daughter of the Queen of the Night in Mozart's
The Magic Flute.

Tosca examines the body of Scarpia, head of the Roman
secret police, whom she has just stabbed in Act Two of
Puccini's *Tosca*.

pears in the score—a sound that was strange to eighteenth-
century audiences. This spot marks the moment when Figaro's
curiosity, or lack of patience, overcomes him. It is a clue for the
stage director in moving his actors.

Such detective work can be used on all kinds of musical theater compositions—in Mozart operas, Offenbach operettas, and

Richard Rodgers musicals, too. Sometimes a composer is un-aware that he is supplying these clues because they occur natu-rally in the writing, in much the same way that people reveal hints about themselves in ordinary conversations through the words and phrases they select.

In opera today, stage directors are occasionally the true stars. A production of La Bohème staged by film director Franco Zeffirelli, or Das Rheingold (The Rhinegold) staged by the young Frenchman Patrice Chéreau, or La Cenerentola (Cinder-ella) staged by designer-director Jean-Pierre Ponnelle may at-tract more attention than the performers. These directors are in-ternational artists who forge the concepts and styles that create sensational stage pictures. They decide whether Parsifal will be played in Edwardian costume and the action set in the London Stock Exchange, or whether Cinderella will dance in an art nouveau ballroom and her coach be a 1903 phaeton brougham.

This current trend in time-warping the classics may have a positive side, however, by focusing attention on several stan-dard operas, warhorses that have for years drawn only flies and dust. These new and flashy productions cause debate and re-crimination, all of which reinforces opera's role as a vital part of the theatrical scene. Even if Violetta's party is given extrava-gant staging and certain bits of interpolated business are booed off the stage, as when a female guest smokes a cigar, or a diner sits next to his pet monkey, La Traviata can withstand the abuse.

The "ship of sails" dominating the harbor is the opera house in Sydney, which in 1973 became the home of the Australian Opera Company.

THE FIRST DIRECTOR OF CARMEN

For the very first production of *Carmen* in Paris in 1875, responsibility for staging was given to Charles Ponchard, a fairly well-known singer in France. He was also a teacher of singing at the Paris Conservatory and the first opera singer to be awarded the esteemed medal from the Legion of Honor. As a stage director, however, he belonged to the old school of traditional staging, and one wonders why such a traditionalist was selected. The realistic nature of the story of *Carmen* called for an understanding of theatrical naturalism that was unknown to a director of Ponchard's training.

There are indications that Bizet had many fights with Ponchard and that Ponchard had problems with the chorus. In all other operas of the period, the chorus was treated as one

massive group that entered as a unit, stood in curved rows, faced the conductor and the audience, and sang. Bizet, however, wanted more naturalistic movement. He wanted the chorus members to enter in twos and threes, to act and interact while they sang. He even wanted some of them to stage quarrels among themselves.

Several of the women in the chorus objected to using lighted cigarettes in the famous "La cloche a sonné," a first-act ensemble depicting the break from their work in the tobacco factory. They complained that they didn't know how to smoke, that it was immoral for women to smoke in public, and that the cigarettes made them sick.

In subsequent productions, many things were changed and,

A nineteenth-century Italian drawing of the tavern of Lillas Pastia in the second act of *Carmen.*

eight years after the premiere in Paris, a revival under a different stage director returned to the traditional school of static staging. He posed his singers in chorus-like groups facing the conductor. The low-life tavern of Lillas Pastia became a respectable hotel where aristocrats sat and watched the performance of a classical ballet, and Carmen was curiously transformed from a down-to-earth gypsy into a chic charmer. The project was doomed—and became laughable when Don José inadvertently dropped his knife while attempting to stab Carmen.

Various liberties have been taken with the staging of *Carmen* over the hundred years of its life. At least fourteen nonmusical motion picture versions have been made since 1909. There was Cecil B. De Mille's silent version with Geraldine Farrar. Theda

Bara starred in another silent version, and Ernst Lubitsch directed Pola Negri in *Gypsy Blood* in 1921. A talkie, *The Loves of Carmen*, was directed by Raoul Walsh, and Dolores Del Rio and Victor McLaglen played the leading roles. The 1948 Hollywood version starred Rita Hayworth. Viviane Romance made a film of *Carmen* in France, and Charlie Chaplin made two separate parodies.

Dramatic stage productions include the Moscow Art Theater's version called *Carmencita and the Soldier*; a Yiddish *Carmen*, which played in New York; a contemporary Puerto Rican version; and Oscar Hammerstein's Broadway musical called *Carmen Jones*, which was later made into a film—both with casts of black performers.

In a recent stage production, when Carmen danced for José in the tavern scene, one imaginative Carmen, finding that she had misplaced her castanets, took a plate off the table, broke it, and used the shards as castanets. In the death scene in another contemporary staging, an innovative Carmen actually pushed herself onto José's dagger, hastening her fate.

Recordings of the musical score of *Carmen* have included a satirical rock version called *The Naked Carmen* by the young American composer John Corigliano. A wildly eccentric transcription for strings and percussion (no winds or brass) has been made by the leading Soviet composer, Rodion Shchedrin, for his wife, Maya Plisetskaya, the prima ballerina of the Bolshoi Theater Ballet. Other ballet companies have staged many versions, including those by choreographers Ruth Page, Roland Petit, and Alicia Alonzo.

The most edifying version I have ever seen was produced recently by the British stage and film director Peter Brook and his experimental theater group in an old vaudeville house, the Théâtre des Bouffes du Nord, in the outskirts of Paris. Brook took the original Mérimée story and the Bizet score and transformed *Carmen* into a stunning eighty-minute, intermissionless musical drama that captured the essence of both story and music with a cast of only four singers and two actors. He trained and rehearsed his entire cast for over a year—all professional opera singers, who became highly trained actors. Their performances were utterly believable. There was no chorus and no ballet. The orchestra consisted of only fifteen players. The arrangements by the skillful composer, Marius Constant, were economic, sparse, yet completely satisfying. When Carmen sang her "Gypsy Song," the accompaniment was a single violin and a tambourine. The orchestra was not missed.

In the production I saw, Carmen was young, lithe, and looked every bit the gypsy. Don José was ruggedly handsome and completely believable. There was no scenery; the action took place on a bare stage in front of an ancient stone wall. The stage floor was covered with red earth and resembled a bullring in its shape. The actors wore simple costumes of blacks and grays. There was no color. When Carmen threw José a small carnation against this somber scene, its redness was stunning by contrast. And when she peeled an orange for him to eat, the color appeared so brilliant that the small object took over the entire stage. After seeing Peter Brook's *Tragedy of Carmen*, I understood and felt more deeply about *Carmen* than I ever had before. It was a production where "less is more."

121

The orchestra pit at the Festspielhaus in Bayreuth, West Germany, built for Richard Wagner and the production of his music dramas. A special feature of the large pit is the cowl, which makes the conductor and the orchestra invisible to the audience.

5
THE CONDUCTOR

Put It All Together

The master of the opera performance is the conductor. Referred to as *maestro* (Italian for "master"), he is, of all the interpreters, the controlling force.

His job begins long before rehearsal, for he must study and virtually memorize the score—both the words and the music. Often preliminary rehearsals are only for the principal singers and are conducted in an informal session around the piano, which the conductor himself may play. Then, little by little, these *sitzprobes* (German for "seated rehearsals") expand to include the entire cast, moving to a large studio where scenery is indicated by lines and shapes painted on the floor, where simple chairs and music stands mark castle walls, a drawbridge, or a portcullis.

If the opera had been unfamiliar to the singers, they have by this time memorized all their music, so there is no need to refer to their scores. The concentration is on their actions and refinement of their vocal interpretations and musical values. In addition to tempo and dynamics, they work on ensemble balance and the problems of line of vision from singer to conductor. Rehearsals enable the conductor to determine how much liberty he can take in stretching out or speeding up musical phrases or in allowing the singer to hold on to the high notes, nuances that make a performance exciting to an audience.

A few days before the final rehearsal, the full orchestra may join the singers and the conductor in a read-through of the opera, especially if it is a rarely performed, new, or unusually difficult work. When it is a complicated orchestral score, there are separate readings held with the conductor and the orchestra, to work together on fine points and interpretation.

In the meantime, the chorus and ballet have been holding separate musical and staging rehearsals. The conductor visits these rehearsals from time to time, helps to coordinate them, and establishes his idea of the overall style of the opera.

The dress rehearsal, which is held on the stage of the opera house, must come as close as possible to an actual performance. Scenery, costumes, makeup, and lighting are all coordinated with the performers on stage and the orchestra in the pit. It is the conductor who is in charge of the amalgamation of the separate parts. Sometimes a small audience is assembled for this

Four views of Gustav Mahler (1860–1911), the great Austrian composer who was principal conductor at the Metropolitan Opera in 1908, and music director of the New York Philharmonic from 1909 to 1911.

rehearsal—usually friends of the cast, sometimes music critics seeking to familiarize themselves with a new work, and sometimes financial contributors or members of associations who support the opera company. Even though this is the final rehearsal before opening night, and even though there are people seated in the audience, some of the singers may not sing in full voice all the time. Singers are trained to save their energy and voices for performances, so they often "mark" their parts by singing softly or in a lower register.

Fitting together all the elements of an opera production is a mammoth undertaking. The forces are multiple and the disciplines are varied. The timing must be precise, and it is the conductor who must coordinate the performances of as many as 250 individual artists.

Certain conductors are able to insist on unusually long and detailed rehearsal schedules. Leonard Bernstein, for example, was given a generous timetable when he opened the Metropolitan Opera season some years ago with a new production of *Carmen;* he was allowed four weeks with the singers and five full rehearsals with the orchestra. Marilyn Horne sang the title role in this special event.

Carlo Maria Giulini, the music director of the Los Angeles Philharmonic, insisted on a rehearsal schedule of several months for a West Coast performance of Verdi's *Falstaff,* with outstanding results. There can never be too much rehearsal. Ex-

cellence in any of the performing arts demands it.

The training of a conductor is arduous, requiring musical as well as nonmusical knowledge. It calls for many technical skills, along with a sensitivity to others and the ability to inspire artists to reach heights of expression they never thought they could.

The conductor's "instrument" is the orchestra, so any practice or honing of his skills requires the presence of thirty-five to one hundred other trained experts. That's just the orchestra. For an opera, add singers, the chorus, the ballet, and the technical staff.

Some well-known conductors not only hold the reins on the musical aspects of a performance, but also direct the staging as well. Julius Rudel, former head of the New York City Opera, and Herbert von Karajan, music director of the Berlin Philharmonic, are two contemporary conductors who have taken on this responsibility.

Other conductors have become legends. When Arturo Toscanini conducted opera during the first half of this century, audiences and critics claimed that nothing like his magic had been heard before. His concept and control of the operas of Verdi and Puccini were without equal. Toscanini had been given his first opportunity to conduct at the early age of nineteen, when he was first cellist of the opera orchestra in Rio de Janeiro. He had been asked to step in for the ailing conductor at a performance of *Aida*, and he conducted the entire score from memory. Several recordings of the many operas he conducted verify his keen talent. He has been called the greatest of the "dictators of the baton." On some early recordings, he can be heard "singing" along with his principal artists. His gruff and nonlyrical voice accompanies all the climaxes, and sometimes even the most delicate passages are underscored with his guttural incantations.

Toscanini continued to conduct without a score. He committed notes and words to memory. Some say he had to do this because his eyesight was so poor that he could not possibly refer to the printed score.

Leopold Stokowski, the most glamourous maestro of the same era, did not perform in the orchestra pit as often as on the concert hall platform. Even while conducting new music, he seldom referred to the *partitur* (the complete orchestral score). He used to say, "The *partitur* is in the head," pointing to his brain. Stokowski, who spent a quarter of a century as musical director of the Philadelphia Orchestra, was an active conductor until the day of his death at age ninety-five in 1977 in London.

Sir Thomas Beecham, a legendary opera and symphony conductor of the first half of this century, was known to enter the orchestra pit immediately before the curtain went up and to casually ask the concertmaster, "What opera are we doing tonight?" When he had received an answer, he would raise his baton and conduct the downbeat for the overture to begin.

As an amateur, I played trumpet and French horn in many orchestras under different professional conductors. Although I have known him for thirty-five years, I never had the opportunity to play in an orchestra under Leonard Bernstein. In preparation for directing a telecast from Mexico City a few years ago, I happened to be on stage during rehearsal, standing next to the tympani player. Bernstein was leading the musicians through Aaron Copland's *El Salón México*. His lively beat, his eagle-eye contact with each section, and his body dancing in time to the music urged each player to give his best. As a leader, Bernstein inspired the most from everyone. Even I, as a bystander, felt the tremendous electricity. He obviously expected more than the players thought they had to give, and he got it, in spite of their limitations. He continues to inspire his musicians, and he achieves incredible results. He reflects the spirit of the music—the supreme talent of a great conductor.

During the two or more hours of nearly any opera performance, all eyes of the cast are on the maestro, including those of the chorus, the ballet, the orchestra, and the principal singers. The conductor sets and maintains the tempi, the dynamics, and the phrasings—all the musical elements of an operatic performance.

The singers are aided in most large opera houses by a prompter, who is hidden from the audience's view by a small hooded shelter built into the footlights at center stage. From this position, he relays the conductor's beat by using a rearview mirror. Softly, yet authoritatively, he calls out the first few words of every phrase a split second before the singer sings it. He provides constant help to the leading singers and has saved many a noted soprano or tenor from complete memory lapse or from having to resort to the invention of a new line in Italian, or a phrase in pig-Latin. The prompter's services are particularly appreciated by the many internationally renowned singers who are called upon to appear as Violetta on Monday, Norma on Wednesday, and Leonora on Friday.

Some of the newer opera houses have installed a more sophisticated system of television cameras. They project a close-up image of the conductor's face and hands on small TV screens, relaying his control and guidance to the offstage chorus and singers backstage and in the wings.

One contemporary conductor, Boris Goldovsky, who also does his own stage directing, places his orchestra *behind* the scenes, where the conductor cannot be seen by either the singers or the audience. His rapport with the cast is so special and he rehearses them so meticulously that the performers' work is unhampered from constant reference to the conductor, and stage action and movement appear flexible and realistic.

No matter where or how the conductor's command is exercised, it is up to every stage performer to heed it. This, however, is only a portion of a well-disciplined performance. The rest is unseen, composed of a feeling, an inspiration that cannot

The prompter responds to the outcries of the audience at an imagined opera performance.

be learned or described because it is transcendent. It is the real magic that takes over the psyches of several hundred people at once—guided by those tiny symbols on a page of music that were written long ago by a composer, and are now interpreted by the conductor.

The first measures of the "Habanera" from Bizet's manuscript score of *Carmen*.

THE ORIGINAL CONDUCTOR OF CARMEN

In all my research on *Carmen*, including countless books and articles, I found only scant mention of the conductor of the original production. I read: "The orchestra, accustomed to the routine scoring of the Auber-Adam school"—two composers of French light opera in the early nineteenth century—"at first resented the greater elaboration and difficulty of Bizet's music, even finding some passages unplayable, and *Deloffre*, the veteran conductor, though a conscientious musician, had little authority."

In another book containing the program listing of the March 3, 1875 premiere, the *chef d'orchestre* is listed merely as M. (Monsieur) *Deloffre*. Not even his first name. Nor was there any background material as to who he was or why he had been chosen to conduct the first performance of this new opera. (I subsequently discovered, however, that this same M. Deloffre had, a few years earlier, conducted the premiere of Bizet's unsuccessful opera, *Djamileh*. A critic's review of that performance reported that "the heroine suddenly skipped thirty-two measures in an aria and the orchestra had to race to catch up with her." Bizet is said to have remarked at the close of this performance, "You can hear the thud. It's a failure.")

The printed vocal and piano score of *Carmen* lists every cast member in the original 1875 production, including the minuscule role of "The Guide." It includes the name of the stage director, but no mention of the conductor. This astounding omission demonstrates how drastically the emphasis can be shifted on the artists' rank of importance in opera. Some years ago, the singers dominated the public interest. Then there was a shift toward the star conductor during the era of Toscanini, Stokowski, Bruno Walter, and Fritz Reiner. At the moment, there is a tendency to emphasize the stage director. Productions by Tito Capobianco, Harold Prince, Frank Corsaro, Jonathan Miller, and John Dexter capture the public's attention. In 1875, at the premiere of *Carmen*, the conductor's star was apparently far below the horizon.

Very little is known about the orchestra at the premiere of *Carmen*. Halévy, the librettist, wrote: "There were difficulties with the orchestra; certain details in the orchestration they declared unplayable, but after more than the usual number of rehearsals, these musicians, excellent on the whole, succeeded in playing what had seemed unplayable." (Again, no mention of the conductor.) It is written that the tympani player, miscounting his bars of rest in the music, shocked the audience— and Carmen, who was softly intoning a subtle passage—by coming in with two loud thumps on his drum.

The first performance of *Carmen* in the United States was conducted by Luigi Arditi, the composer of the well-known

An old poster for *Carmen* with a scene from the final act, when Don José challenges Carmen outside the bullring.

concert piece, the vocal waltz "Il Bacio." In our own time, Leonard Bernstein's conducting of *Carmen* at the Metropolitan drew highest praise from audience and critics alike. In fact, it was this production in 1972 that brought the original version of the opera to the Met for the first time—the version with the spoken dialogue as Bizet had initially conceived and written it.

133

The audience at the Royal Opera House, Covent Garden, London, home of the Royal Opera and the Royal Ballet.

PART THREE

THE APPRECIATORS

Part of the audience in the nineteen-hundred-seat Deutsche
Oper Berlin, a clean-lined modern structure that opened its
doors in 1961.

6
THE AUDIENCE AND THE CRITICS

The Piper Must Be Paid

If a tree falls in the forest and no one is there to hear it, is a sound produced? This philosophical puzzle applies to a theatrical performance at which there is no audience.

The audience is the largest group of the three essential components in the making of music and the making of an opera.

People pay their money, whether at a theater box office, a record store, or by buying advertised products mentioned on radio and television commercials. Audiences are made up of professional musicians, passionate music lovers, doctors, lawyers, students, and in general, all sorts of people. And each one is a critic.

A good audience is a knowledgeable audience. European opera audiences are thought to be harder to please than those in

An engraving of the audience in the opera house at the
Vienna Hofburg in the seventeenth century.

America. The Viennese opera audience has been called the
toughest in the world. Italian audiences, especially in the prov-
inces, are the most passionate in their praise and the most vehe-
ment in their disapproval.

Audiences have not always displayed the manners we see today. Only for the last hundred years or so has opera been performed in darkened theaters. Before the advent of electrical

stage lighting, chandeliers brightened the auditorium, and vendors hawked food and beverages throughout the evening. The members of the audience would judge each other's attire, chat among themselves, parade in and out of the hall continuously, and give their full attention to the performers only during some riveting action on stage.

Richard Wagner was chiefly responsible for changes in manners. He and conductors after him—especially Gustav Mahler and Arturo Toscanini—insisted that lights be focused only on the stage during performances.

Even today audiences sometimes interrupt the musical flow, their shouts of approval or applause breaking into the last few bars of an aria. If the performance is unusually good, an appreciative "Bravo!" (which in Italian means "Hooray," or "You've done well!") is heard for the male singers; "Brava!" is heard for the female singers, or "Bravi!" for both of them. The word "Bis!" is sometimes shouted if the performance is especially fine. That means "twice" in Latin and, like the word "encore" in French, means "We want to hear it again." In days past, some opera houses respected a tradition of repeating an aria if the audience insisted.

Some singers have hired people to lead applause and cheers in order to insure an approving audience response. These low-paid but operatically knowledgeable attendees are distributed in all parts of the opera house. They are called claques, from the French word claquer, "to clap." Theirs is not considered an honorable profession, and fortunately they are not much in evidence today.

On the other hand, clear evidence of disapproval at what takes place on stage is often seen and heard. In Italy, especially in Parma and Verona, loud disruptive "boos" are sometimes heard at the end of arias, and rolled-up programs are thrown. Even tomatoes are tossed at the singers. Many performers have been stopped by such interruptions, and leading divas occa-

139

sionally refuse to continue a performance when the amount of vegetables on the stage floor makes walking dangerous.

Backstage, before a performance begins, singers are greeted by their friends and colleagues with certain traditional theatrical phrases conveying best wishes and good luck, such as "Break a leg." The phrase "Good luck" is never uttered before a performance. That would surely bring disaster.

Well-wishers who speak Italian often greet artists in their dressing rooms with the phrase "In bocca al lupo" ("In the mouth of the wolf"), which is probably a shortened version of the full statement meaning "You're going to be in the most vulnerable place imaginable, but my wish will give you forewarning and strength." Historically, this strange phrase originates from the architectural feature of most small European opera houses, whose balcony seats are set in rows of semi-circles and, when viewed from the stage, look like rows of teeth—like "the mouth of the wolf."

And you, as a member of the audience, have the privilege of judging for yourself whether or not you like the performance, whether to shout bravo and applaud enthusiastically or to express your disapproval by withholding applause or by some other signal. Whether a new operagoer or a seasoned buff, you should question your reactions: Do I like this? What do I like about this performance? What don't I like about it? Such questioning sharpens your critical faculties and helps to dispel some of the mystery of any work of art.

An easy way to begin to understand a work and to acquire critical perception is to read reviews by professional critics in newspapers and magazines. Compare your thoughts with theirs. Even if you do not agree, most critics are trained to think logically, and they possess background knowledge of the many styles and forms of music and its production.

Harold Clurman, who was an outstanding man of the American theater—director, author, critic, and teacher—said, "A critic should know the major works of drama of almost all nations, from the Greeks to contemporary drama. He should know the history of theater, and literature in general—from Homer on. He should also read the very best critics of literature and drama from Aristotle to Hazlitt to Shaw. He should know a good deal about music, dance, architecture, painting, world history, and the history of his country. He should know people. To judge acting, you must be able to judge people. He should have a philosophy, an attitude toward life.''

Even though Clurman was talking about qualities for a drama critic, these same requirements are necessary for an opera critic or for an intelligent member of an opera audience.

One of the finest critics writing today is Walter Kerr of *The New York Times*. He covers the theater and each week he writes about some broad question that relates to the current Broadway scene. Yet he peppers his commentary with references to recent productions and performances. His way of bringing a performance to the eye is the most exciting quality of Kerr's writing. In his description of a play or a musical, he has the ability to pick out exactly the right detail to recreate the event, enabling the reader to feel he is in the theater watching.

This lively "you are there" approach is only a part of Kerr's brilliance in expounding on overall issues of playwriting, directing, acting, and production. A good reviewer can enlarge his reader's scope and understanding of an art form. He can provide corroboration for an audience's intuitive criticisms that most individuals are unable to recognize or express. A good critic can instruct theatrical creators in how to refine and improve their craft. In short, responsible and insightful critics supply a valuable service to the theater.

Among contemporary music critics who regularly review opera, three are outstanding. Leighton Kerner, who writes in New York's *Village Voice*, shares Walter Kerr's "you are there" approach and has a vast knowledge of all kinds of music. Alan

Rich of Los Angeles, who formerly wrote for the magazine *New York*, expresses some very outspoken and interesting opinions of things musical in a breezy and readable style. And Andrew Porter, writing for *The New Yorker* magazine, is certainly a thorough researcher and a critic who has a knack of getting to the heart of the matter with carefully chosen words. Porter is currently supplying opera producers with highly intelligent English translations of standard works, and has embarked on a new career: directing operas he has translated. He recently commented on his dual role as critic and sometime director while staging *The Abduction from the Seraglio:* "[This experience] has sharpened a sense of the opera's richness and of varied possibilities in its execution and has increased [my] tolerance of what goes wrong, and impatience with what can be put right."

The art of serious music criticism has a long and distinguished history. It became popular with the advent of daily newspapers and periodicals. Its most illustrious practitioners have included composers themselves writing about other composers: Robert Schumann, Carl Maria von Weber, Hector Berlioz, Franz Liszt, Hugo Wolf, Wagner, and Debussy. The literary giant E. T. A. Hoffmann, whose stories formed the basis of Offenbach's opera *The Tales of Hoffmann*, was a well-known music critic. Walt Whitman, the American poet who lived during the time of the American Civil War, was an avid operagoer and wrote a critical book about it. George Bernard Shaw, the British dramatist, wrote music criticism under the assumed name "Corno Di Bassetto" (an obsolete Italian musical instrument). The nineteenth-century American composer William Henry Fry wrote for *The New York Herald Tribune;* and in the twentieth century, Virgil Thomson, the composer of the milestone opera *Four Saints in Three Acts,* was chief music critic for that same newspaper. In fact, Thomson, when asked about the variance in critical opinions of the same piece of music or the

A formal informality at a between-the-acts picnic on the lawns at Glyndebourne, England, where the audiences enjoy superlative opera performances.

same performance of it, said, "Nobody has to be right."

There are no right or wrong answers in matters of taste. What appeals to you may not appeal to everyone else. Yet there are certain aesthetic principles that apply to both the creation and the interpretation of a work of art.

As a student at the University of Chicago, I learned three simple rules. It was always a confusing mystery why I enjoyed certain operas more than others. Apart from the subject matter and style of the composer or the production, there seemed to be no way of testing my reasons for liking one work over another until a fellow operagoer and friend, Rowena Morse Mann, showed me a method. Dr. Mann was a professor in the philosophy department and had specialized in aesthetics, the branch of philosophy that pertains to the study of beauty in art. She would ask simply, "Does the work in question contain these elements?"

UNITY—focus and order of all the elements; a unifying structure contained within a framework.

VARIETY—a diversity of contrasting characters and events, moods and emotions.

TRUTH—a sense of rightness, a universality that makes it ring true to human nature and experience.

If a work contains these three elements, it is well crafted.

The Library of Congress in Washington, D. C., contains over twenty-five thousand different opera scores, which is considered to be only about two-thirds of the world's output. Of course, many of these operas exist only in manuscript form, have not been published, and have never been presented on stage. Add to this the fact that every year, in the United States alone, nearly a hundred and fifty new opera scores are created, and perhaps only a half dozen ever see the opera stage.

Great operas are rare. Audiences and critics have determined from their responses over the years which ones survive. The handful that are seen today have withstood the test of time.

When one considers that the art form is four hundred years old, and that over forty thousand operas have been written in that period, it is a hard fact of life that today fewer than one hundred remain in the world's popular repertoire, with perhaps another one hundred given an occasional performance. At best, that make one half of one percent.

Le Théâtre National de l'Opéra-Comique, the Salle Favart, built in Paris in 1840, the building in which *Carmen* was created and first staged in 1875. This pen drawing by A. Deroy shows the building's destruction by a fire in 1887.

CARMEN, OPENING NIGHT

The audience on the night of March 3, 1875, was star-studded. It included the famous composers Charles Gounod (*Faust*), Ambroise Thomas (*Mignon*), Léo Delibes (*Lakmé*), Jacques Offenbach (*The Tales of Hoffmann*), Jules Massenet (*Manon*), Charles LeCocq (*Giroflé-Girofla*), and Vincent D'Indy (a composer of concert music). Also present were the writers Alphonse and Ernest Daudet (novelist and dramatist brothers), and Alexandre Dumas *fils* (author of *Camille*), along with Prince Troubetskoi, a Russian nobleman, and a notable assembly of music publishers and music critics. Naturally, the fashionable world of Paris was there as well.

As the opera progressed, the audience's reactions grew cooler and cooler. What had started as a general excitement at the ends of Acts I and II became less animated at the end of the next act, and finally dwindled to silence at the end of the opera. The realism was too much for the audience to accept.

The reviews that followed in the French press were generally unfavorable. One noted critic said that the subject was far too obscene to be staged. Another said that Galli-Marié "overemphasized the seamy side of her role to such an extent that to go much further would provoke the intervention of the police." Still another commented that "[she] should be gagged, a stop put to the twisting of her hips; she should be fastened into a straitjacket after being cooled off by a jug of water poured over her head." The review went on, "Micaëla is the only decent and sympathetic character in the midst of this inferno of ridiculous and uninteresting corruption."

Other reviewers said, "Carmen is neither scenic nor dramatic," and, "The music is anything but original and lacks distinction."

Not all the reviews, however, were negative. There were a few favorable comments: "Bizet is one of those ambitious men for whom music must be not an entertainment, but a divine language. He tried to show real men and women tortured by passion. . . ." Not what one would call a good box office review. But at least the critic was sympathetic to the composer's intention.

Bizet was devastated by the negative criticism. It was reported that after the theater was empty, he and his friend Ernest Guiraud, who wrote the recitatives for the later productions, walked the streets of Paris in great depression until dawn.

It is probably overdramatic to assume that Bizet's premature death at age thirty-seven was due to the failure of Carmen and the poor response of both audience and critics. Yet one may assume that the stress of rehearsals and the worry brought on by the creative pressure made him a target for an illness he might have survived in better mental and physical state. He suffered a

CARMEN

H. MEILHAC L. HALÉVY   GEORGES BIZET

severe attack of angina several weeks later, and his slow recovery was accompanied by a throat inflammation and severe mental depression. On June 3, three months after the premiere, he died in his sleep.

Oddly enough, *Carmen* encouraged the realistic movement in opera that had already been stirring in Italy known as *verismo*, meaning "truth" (or, more accurately, "realism"), the style that has remained the most popular with audiences to this day.

Sadly, Bizet never lived to see the success of his masterpiece or to receive the plaudits of his fans, who grew to include the philosopher Friedrich Nietzsche, Chancellor Bismarck of the German Empire, and virtually every composer living then or now. Wagner said, "Here at last, thank God, is someone with ideas in his head." Brahms saw twenty performances of *Carmen* and said he would have gone to the ends of the earth to embrace Bizet. Tchaikovsky proclaimed *Carmen* a masterpiece and predicted that within ten years it would be the most popular opera in the world.

149

One of the two large workrooms at the Berlin Opera House where
scenery is painted and refurbished for new productions.

EPILOGUE

The Future of Opera

Opera, being the most complicated of the arts in that it incorporates so many diverse elements, is also the most expensive to present. At the Metropolitan Opera House in New York City, there are twenty-two unions involved in just one operatic performance. The singers, stage directors, chorus, and ballet are represented by the American Guild of Musical Artists (AGMA); the orchestral musicians are represented by the American Federation of Musicians (AF of M); the scenery, costume, and lighting designers by the United Scenic Artists (USA); the stagehands by the International Alliance of Theatrical Stage Employees (IATSE); the press and publicity people, as well as the box office staff, by the Association of Theatrical Press Agents and Managers (ATPAM); the contemporary composers

and librettists by the American Society of Composers, Authors, and Publishers (ASCAP) or Broadcast Music Inc. (BMI); and the wardrobe attendants, ticket takers, ushers, engineers, and cleaning personnel by other unions and associations. Every year or so, spokesmen for these employees negotiate new contracts demanding increased wages. In turn, ticket prices go up. Because of these financial pressures, it becomes increasingly problematic to mount an opera.

Cost is not the only difficult aspect of production. Scheduling of musical coaching, staging rehearsals, costume fittings, and even photographic and publicity sessions, present a jigsaw puzzle that nearly defies solution. During the height of the season in any opera house, space and time are apportioned and dovetailed carefully. A singer in *Madama Butterfly* must be released from staging rehearsals in time for her coaching session with an assistant conductor for her scheduled role in *Rigoletto* and still have time to rest before her performance that same night in *The Tales of Hoffmann*.

Following the nightly performance, a busy opera house is seldom empty or quiet. Activity continues around the clock. Well

An outdoor production of Puccini's last opera, *Turandot,* an oriental spectacle. From an Indiana University production.

after midnight, long after the cleaning staff has left, scenery is constructed and painted. Stage space, at a premium during the day for lighting and technical rehearsals, may be used at night as a painting studio by artists who bring the scenic designer's sketches to life in true scale.

Experts in scheduling are on the staff of opera management, along with personnel who handle contracts, press and publicity, fund raising, (euphemistically called "development"), ticket sales, and technical stage departments. All these people function under the direction of a general manager or, in some companies, an artistic director, who may be also the leading conductor.

The kind of opera we have been discussing—grand opera—is merely a step along the continuous line called musical theater that stretches back to the Greek dramas, the early Camerata experiments in Florence, the singspiel, the operetta, and the modern American musical comedy. This continuum, stretching along five thousand years of history, is constantly shifting and changing, borrowing old forms to augment the new, and inventing additions to heighten the effectiveness of the art.

It is ironic that the roots and meanings of the words used to label our two principal theatrical entertainments have curious connotations. *Opera* is the plural of the Latin word *opus*, meaning "work." In the theater, a drama is called a *play*. Work versus play!—it doesn't seem fair. Audiences do not have to work to enjoy an opera any more than to enjoy a play.

Operas are not "difficult." Like plays, they present stories for the entertainment of an audience. In order to be worthy, operas must communicate the sense and feeling of the story to the audience.

Many operatic masterpices are based on great plays: *Othello, The Marriage of Figaro, Porgy and Bess, Pélleas et Mélisande,* and *Wozzeck*. Others—*La Gioconda, Il Trovatore, Mignon,* and *Norma*—have ridiculous plots, yet despite their texts have become successful operas.

With today's sophisticated and discriminating audiences, it would be good insurance to try out an original libretto for a new opera as a spoken stage play *without* music. If the play holds the audience's interest, then the addition of the music should enhance its theatricality.

Looking at opera in the context of the history of musical theater, a clear view emerges of its growing democratization and its widening appeal. When opera was first "invented" in Florence in 1580, it was presented in royal courts for the elite. In Europe it broadened its audience to include the lesser nobility. When it moved into still larger opera houses in America, it became a public entertainment available to everyone. With the advent of radio broadcasting, phonograph and tape recording, it expanded the confines of the auditorium. With television and home video equipment, its reaches are unlimited. What might operas of the future be like? They will continue to be an amalgam of music and drama, but they will be told with the aid of new technical and creative means.

New York University, for instance, has recently inaugurated

a graduate department of musical theater for composers, librettists, and lyricists who have written for the musical stage. They study under experienced and successful practitioners of their art, and these master teachers advise their students in creating original works for the musical theater.

Any writing for the musical stage is a collaborative process. In history's list of great masterpieces, only a handful of composers—Wagner, Menotti, Shostakovich, Berg, and Boito—wrote both words and music for their operas. The overwhelming majority of composers counted on receiving a daily manuscript of lyrics and scenes from their collaborators.

In the future, creators of Broadway theater scores and concert music—Leonard Bernstein, Stephen Sondheim, John Corigliano, Thomas Pasatieri, Carlisle Floyd, Philip Glass, and others yet unknown—will create new forms to entertain and enrich, merging their talents with those of writers of contemporary novels, poems, plays, films, television drama, and perhaps even comic-book stories, to create theatrical excitement beyond our present experience.

The best operas, as Andrew Porter suggests, seem to be created when the composer is suddenly seized by a subject in a blinding flash and rushes to set down notes without delay. As Verdi once put it, this inspiration enables the composer to say: "That's it! That's the one!"

Writers and composers can turn the "not yet" into reality. It is in their creations of design, dance, drama, and music that we are given a glimpse not of what *is*, but of what *could be*.

Perhaps you can now see what the screaming is all about—it is a grateful response to the grandest art of all.

APPENDIXES

I

LEADING COMPOSERS

(IN ALPHABETICAL ORDER)

BARBER, SAMUEL
b. West Chester, Penn., 1910. d. New York, 1981.
Vanessa; Antony and Cleopatra; A Hand of Bridge.

BEETHOVEN, LUDWIG VAN
b. Bonn, 1770. d. Vienna, 1827.
Fidelio.

BELLINI, VINCENZO
b. Catania, 1801. d. Puteaux, 1835.
Norma; La Sonnambula; I Puritani; Il Pirata; Beatrice di Tenda.

BERG, ALBAN
b. Vienna, 1885. d. Vienna, 1935.
Wozzeck; Lulu.

BERLIOZ, HECTOR
b. Côte-Saint-André, 1803. d. Paris, 1869.
Les Troyens; La Damnation de Faust; Béatrice et Bénédict; Benvenuto Cellini.

BIZET, GEORGES
b. Paris, 1838. d. Bougival, 1875.
Carmen; Les Pêcheurs de perles; La Jolie fille de Perth;
Djamileh; Le Docteur Miracle.

BOITO, ARRIGO
b. Padua, 1842. d. Milan, 1918.
Mefistofele; Nerone; Orestiade; Ero and Leandro.

BORODIN, ALEXANDER
b. St. Petersburg, 1833. d. St. Petersburg, 1887.
Prince Igor; The Bogatyrs; Mlada.

BRITTEN, BENJAMIN
b. Lowestoft, 1913. d. Aldeburgh, 1976.
Peter Grimes; The Turn of the Screw; Death in Venice;
Albert Herring; Billy Budd; The Rape of Lucretia.

CHARPENTIER, GUSTAVE
b. Dieuze, 1860. d. Paris, 1956.
Louise; Julien.

DEBUSSY, CLAUDE
b. St.-Germain-en-Laye, 1862. d. Paris, 1918.
Pelléas et Mélisande.

DELIBES, LEO
b. St.-Germain-du-Val, 1836. d. Paris, 1891.
Lakmé; Le Roi l'a dit; Jean de Nivelle; Kassya.

DONIZETTI, GAETANO
b. Bergamo, 1797. d. Bergamo, 1848.
Lucia di Lammermoor; L'Elisir d'Amore; Don Pasquale;
Anna Bolena; Maria Stuarda.

GERSHWIN, GEORGE
b. Brooklyn, 1898. d. Hollywood, 1937.
Porgy and Bess; 125th Street; Of Thee I Sing; Let 'Em Eat Cake; Strike Up the Band.

GIORDANO, UMBERTO
b. Foggia, 1867. d. Milan, 1948.
Andrea Chénier; Fedora; Madame Sans-Gêne; Il Re; Siberia.

GLUCK, CHRISTOPH WILLIBALD
b. Erasbach, 1714. d. Vienna, 1787.
Orfeo ed Euridice; Alceste; Iphigénie en Aulide; Armide; Iphigénie en Tauride.

GOUNOD, CHARLES
b. Paris, 1818. d. Saint-Cloud, 1893.
Faust; Roméo et Juliette; Mireille; Sapho; La Reine de Saba.

HANDEL, GEORGE FREDERICK
b. Halle, 1685. d. London, 1759.
Giulio Cesare in Egitto; Il Pastor Fido; Rinaldo; Rodelinda; Ottone; Alcina.

HUMPERDINCK, ENGELBERT
b. Siegburg, 1854. d. Neustrelitz, 1921.
Hänsel und Gretel; Die Königskinder; Die sieben Geislein; Dornröschen; Die Marketenderin.

LEONCAVALLO, RUGGIERO
b. Naples, 1858. d. Florence, 1919.
I Pagliacci; Chatterton; Zazà; La Bohème; I Zingari.

MASCAGNI, PIETRO
b. Leghorn, 1863. d. Rome, 1945.
Cavalleria Rusticana; L'Amico Fritz; Iris; Lodoletta; Il Piccolo Marat.

MASSENET, JULES
b. Montaud, 1842. d. Paris, 1912.
Manon; Thaïs; Esclarmonde; Le Cid; Hérodiade; Werther.

MENOTTI, GIAN CARLO
b. Cadegliano, 1911.
The Consul; The Medium; Amahl and the Night Visitors;
Amelia Goes to the Ball; The Saint of Bleecker Street.

MEYERBEER, GIACOMO
b. Berlin, 1791. d. Paris, 1864.
Les Huguenots; L'Africaine; Le Prophète; Dinorah;
Robert le diable.

MONTEVERDI, CLAUDIO
(Wrote earliest operas still produced)
b. Cremona, 1567. d. Venice, 1643.
L'Incoronazione di Poppea; Il Ballo delle Ingrate; Il
Combattimento di Tancredi e Clorinda; La Favola d'Orfeo.

MOZART, WOLFGANG AMADEUS
b. Salzburg, 1756. d. Vienna, 1791.
Don Giovanni; Le Nozze di Figaro; Così fan Tutte;
Die Zauberflöte; Idomeneo; La Clemenza di Tito;
Die Entführung aus dem Serail.

MUSSORGSKY, MODEST
b. Karevo, Pskov, 1839. d. St. Petersburg, 1881.
Boris Godunov; Khovanshchina; The Fair at Sorochinsk;
Salammbô; Mlada.

OFFENBACH, JACQUES
b. Cologne, 1819. d. Paris, 1880.
Les Contes d'Hoffmann; La Belle Hélène; Barbe-bleue; La Vie
Parisienne; La Périchole.

PONCHIELLI, AMILCARE
b. Cremona, 1834. d. Milan, 1886.
La Gioconda; Il Figliuol Prodigo; I Promessi Sposi; Roderico;
La Savoiarda.

POULENC, FRANCIS
b. Paris, 1899. d. Paris, 1963.
Les Mamelles de Tirésias; Les Dialogues des Carmélites;
La Voix Humaine.

PROKOFIEV, SERGEI
b. Sontzovka, 1891. d. Moscow, 1953.
The Love of Three Oranges; The Flaming Angel; The Gambler;
War and Peace; The Duenna.

PUCCINI, GIACOMO
b. Lucca, 1858. d. Brussels, 1924.
La Bohème; Tosca; Madama Butterfly; Turandot;
Manon Lescaut; Il Trittico (Il Tabarro, Suor Angelica, Gianni
Schicchi).

PURCELL, HENRY
b. London, 1659. d. London, 1695.
Dido and Aeneas; The Fairy Queen; King Arthur;
The Prophetess; The Indian Queen.

RAVEL, MAURICE
b. Ciboure, 1875. d. Paris, 1937.
L'Heure espagnole; L'Enfant et les Sortilèges.

RIMSKY-KORSAKOV, NIKOLAI
b. Tikhvin, 1844. d. Lyubensk, 1908.
Le Coq d'or; A May Night; The Snow Maiden; Sadko;
Christmas Eve.

ROSSINI, GIOACCHINO
b. Pesaro, 1792. d. Paris, 1868.
Il Barbiere di Siviglia; Guillaume Tell; La Cenerentola; L'Italiana in Algeri; Il Turco in Italia.

SAINT-SAENS, CAMILLE
b. Paris, 1835. d. Algiers, 1921.
Samson et Dalila; Ascanio; Henri VIII; La Princesse jaune; Hélène.

SHOSTAKOVICH, DMITRI
b. St. Petersburg, 1906. d. Moscow, 1975.
The Nose; Lady Macbeth of Mtsensk; Moskva Cheryomushki; The Gambler.

SMETANA, BEDRICH
b. Litomyschl, 1824. d. Prague, 1884.
The Bartered Bride; Dalibor; The Kiss; Libuše; The Two Widows.

STRAUSS, JOHANN
b. Vienna, 1825. d. Vienna, 1899.
Die Fledermaus; Der Zigeunerbaron; A Night in Venice; Cagliostro; Carnival in Rome.

STRAUSS, RICHARD
b. Munich, 1864. d. Garmisch-Partenkirchen, 1949.
Der Rosenkavalier; Salome; Elektra; Ariadne auf Naxos; Arabella; Die Frau ohne Schatten.

STRAVINSKY, IGOR
b. Oranienbaum, 1882. d. New York, 1971.
Le Rossignol; The Rake's Progress; Mavra; Oedipus Rex.

SULLIVAN, SIR ARTHUR
b. London, 1842. d. London, 1900.
The Pirates of Penzance; HMS Pinafore; Iolanthe; The Gondoliers; The Mikado.

TCHAIKOVSKY, PETER ILYICH
b. Votkinsk, 1840. d. St. Petersburg, 1893.
Eugene Onegin; The Queen of Spades; Iolanthe; Mazeppa; The Maid of Orleans.

THOMAS, AMBROISE
b. Metz, 1811. d. Paris, 1896.
Mignon; Hamlet; Raymond; Le Caïd; Psyché.

THOMSON, VIRGIL
b. Kansas City, 1896.
Four Saints in Three Acts; The Mother of Us All; Lord Byron.

VERDI, GIUSEPPE
b. Busseto, 1813. d. Milan, 1901.
La Traviata; Il Trovatore; Aida; Otello; Falstaff; Rigoletto; Un Ballo in Maschera; La Forza del Destino.

WAGNER, RICHARD
b. Leipzig, 1813. d. Venice, 1883.
Tristan und Isolde; Lohengrin; Tännhauser; Parsifal; Der Ring des Nibelungen (Das Rheingold, Die Walküre, Siegfried, Götterdämmerung).

WEBER, CARL MARIA VON
b. Eutin, Lübeck, 1786. d. London, 1826.
Der Freischütz; Oberon; Euryanthe; Abu Hassan; Die drei Pintos.

WOLF-FERRARI, ERMANNO
b. Venice, 1876. d. Venice, 1948.
I Quattro Rusteghi; Il Segreto di Susanna; Sly; I Gioiello della Madonna; Le Donne Curiose.

165

II
LEADING LIBRETTISTS

BARBIER, JULES
b. Paris, 1822. d. Paris, 1901.
Faust (Gounod); *Mignon* (Thomas); *Roméo et Juliette* (Gounod);
Les Contes d'Hoffmann (Offenbach); *Dinorah* (Meyerbeer).

BOITO, ARRIGO
b. Padua, 1842. d. Milan, 1918.
Falstaff (Verdi); *Otello* (Verdi); *La Gioconda* (Ponchielli);
Mefistofele (Boito); *Nerone* (Boito).

BRECHT, BERTOLT
b. Augsberg, 1898. d. Berlin, 1956.
The Three Penny Opera (Weill); *Rise and Fall of the City of Mahagonny* (Weill); *Happy End* (Weill); *Der Jasager* (Weill).

BUSENELLO, GIOVANNI
b. Venice, 1598. d. Venice, 1659.
L'Incoronazione di Poppea (Monteverdi); *Statira* (Cavalli);
Gli Amori d'Apollo e di Dafne (Cavalli); *Didone* (Cavalli).

CAMMARANO, SALVATORE
b. Naples, 1801. d. Naples, 1852.
Lucia di Lammermoor (Donizetti); *Don Pasquale* (Donizetti); *Il Trovatore* (Verdi); *Luisa Miller* (Verdi); *Alzira* (Verdi).

CARRE, MICHEL
b. Paris, 1819. d. Argenteuil, 1872.
Faust (Gounod); *Mignon* (Thomas); *Roméo et Juliette* (Gounod); *Hamlet* (Thomas); *Les Contes d'Hoffmann* (Offenbach).

DA PONTE, LORENZO
b. Venice, 1749. d. New York, 1838.
Don Giovanni (Mozart); *Le Nozze di Figaro* (Mozart); *Così fan Tutte* (Mozart); *Il Ricco d'un Giorno* (Salieri).

FORZANO, GIOVACCHINO
b. Borgo San Lorenzo, 1883. d. Rome, 1970.
Suor Angelica (Puccini); *Gianni Schicchi* (Puccini); *Sly* (Wolf-Ferrari); *Lodoletto* (Mascagni); *Il Piccolo Marat* (Mascagni).

GIACOSA, GIUSEPPE
b. Colleretto-Parella, 1847. d. Turin, 1906.
La Bohème (Puccini); *Tosca* (Puccini); *Madama Butterfly* (Puccini).

GILBERT, WILLIAM SCHWENK
b. London, 1836. d. Harrow Weald, Middlesex, 1911.
The Pirates of Penzance (Sullivan); *Iolanthe* (Sullivan); *The Mikado* (Sullivan); *The Gondoliers* (Sullivan); *HMS Pinafore* (Sullivan).

GOLDONI, CARLO
b. Venice, 1707. d. Paris, 1793.
Il Mondo della Luna (Haydn); *La Finta Semplice* (Mozart); *Tigrane* (Gluck); *I Quattro Rusteghi* (Wolf-Ferrari).

HALEVY, LUDOVIC
b. Paris, 1834. d. Paris, 1908.
Carmen (Bizet); La Belle Hélène (Offenbach);
La Périchole (Offenbach); Orphée aux Enfers (Offenbach);
Die Fledermaus (Strauss).

HOFMANNSTHAL, HUGO VON
b. Vienna, 1874. d. Vienna, 1929.
Der Rosenkavalier (Strauss); Ariadne auf Naxos (Strauss);
Elektra (Strauss); Die Frau ohne Schatten (Strauss).

ILLICA, LUIGI
b. Castellarquato, 1857. d. Castellarquato, 1919.
La Bohème (Puccini); Tosca (Puccini); Madama Butterfly
(Puccini); Andrea Chénier (Giordano); Iris (Mascagni);
La Wally (Catalani).

MEILHAC, HENRI
b. Paris, 1831. d. Paris, 1897.
Carmen (Bizet); Manon (Massenet); La Belle Hélène
(Offenbach); Barbe-bleue (Offenbach); La Vie Parisienne
(Offenbach).

MENOTTI, GIAN CARLO
b. Cadegliano, 1911.
The Consul (Menotti); The Medium (Menotti); Amahl and the
Night Visitors (Menotti); Amelia Goes to the Ball (Menotti);
Vanessa (Barber).

METASTASIO, PIETRO
b. Rome, 1698. d. Vienna, 1782.
La Clemenza di Tito (Mozart); L'Isola Disabitata (Haydn);
Il Sogno di Scipione (Mozart); Semiramide (Meyerbeer).

PIAVE, FRANCESCO
b. Mureno, 1810. d. Milan, 1876.
La Traviata (Verdi); *Rigoletto* (Verdi); *Simon Boccanegra* (Verdi); *Macbeth* (Verdi); *La Forza del Destino* (Verdi); *Ernani* (Verdi).

RINUCCINI, OTTAVIO
(The first librettist)
b. Florence, 1562. d. Florence, 1621.
L'Arianna (Monteverdi); *Il Ballo delle Ingrate* (Monteverdi); *Dafne* (Peri); *Euridice* (Peri).

ROMANI, FELICE
b. Genoa, 1788. d. Moneglia, Riviera, 1865.
Norma (Bellini); *La Sonnambula* (Bellini); *Un Giorno di Regno* (Verdi); *L'Elisir d'Amore* (Donizetti); *Il Turco in Italia* (Rossini).

SCRIBE, EUGENE
b. Paris, 1791. d. Paris, 1861.
Les Huguenots (Meyerbeer); *La Juive* (Halévy); *Le Comte Ory* (Rossini); *Il Duca d'Alba* (Donizetti); *Fra Diavolo* (Auber).

WAGNER, RICHARD
b. Leipzig, 1813. d. Venice, 1883.
Tristan und Isolde; Lohengrin; Tännhauser; Parsifal; Der Ring des Nibelungen (Das Rheingold, Die Walküre, Siegfried, Götterdämmerung).

III
LEADING OPERA COMPANIES

UNITED STATES
 New York
  Metropolitan Opera
  New York City Opera
 Illinois
  Chicago Lyric Opera
 California
  San Francisco Opera
  San Diego Opera
 Texas
  Houston Grand Opera
  Dallas Civic Opera
 New Mexico
  Santa Fe Opera Festival
 Washington
  Seattle Opera
 District of Columbia
  Washington Opera
 Massachusetts
  Opera Society of Boston

GREAT BRITAIN

Royal Opera, Covent Garden, London
Glyndebourne Festival
Scottish Opera, Glasgow
Welsh National Opera, Cardiff

FRANCE

Paris Opéra
Opéra-Comique of Paris

ITALY

La Scala, Milan
Rome Opera
San Carlo Opera, Naples

GERMANY

Berlin Opera
Bavarian State Opera, Munich
Frankfurt Opera
Hamburg Opera
Bayreuth Festival

AUSTRIA

Vienna State Opera
Salzburg Festival

RUSSIA

Bolshoi Opera, Moscow
Kirov Opera, Leningrad

AUSTRALIA

Australian Opera, Sydney

MEXICO

Bellas Artes, Mexico City

SOUTH AMERICA

Teatro Colón, Buenos Aires, Argentina

IV
GLOSSARY

ALEATORY MUSIC
> music of chance or unpredictability in either its composition or performance; sometimes referred to as "dice music"

ALTO See CONTRALTO

APPOGGIATURA
> a note inserted between two other notes giving emphasis or elegance to a melodic progression

APRON
> the part of the stage in front of the proscenium arch

ARIA
> a composition for solo voice with instrumental accompaniment, from the Greek *aer*, meaning "air"

ATONALITY
> the absence of tonality

BACKDROP
> a painted curtain hung at the back of a stage set

BALLAD OPERA
> a form of stage entertainment originating in eighteenth-century England, where spoken dialogue alternates with popular music taken from ballad tunes and folk songs

BALLET
> a theatrical presentation with musical accompaniment performed by a group of dancers, usually with costumes and scenery

BARITONE
> the male voice lying between the bass and tenor range

BAROQUE
> the music of the period 1600–1750, characterized by an elaborately embellished style as contrasted to the simplicity of the Renaissance style

BASS
> the male voice of the lowest range

BASSO BUFFO
> a bass singer who portrays comic characters, especially in eighteenth-century opera

BASSO PROFUNDO
> a male singer with the lowest bass range and a voice of power and solemn character

BATON
> a French word that refers to the slender wooden stick used by a conductor to direct an orchestra

BEL CANTO
> the Italian vocal technique of the eighteenth century, with total emphasis on beauty of sound

BRAVO
> a shout of approval from the audience

CABALETTA
> a song in an opera with a uniform vocal rhythm and accompaniment

CADENZA
> a composed or improvised passage of varying length that demonstrates the artist's virtuosity

CAMERATA
> the group of writers and musicians who met in the palace of Count Bardi in Florence around 1580, and whose discussions and experiments led to the creation of the musical-dramatic form of opera

CANTATA
> a composition for voice containing such movements as arias, recitatives, duets, and choruses based on a narrative text, and usually staged

CANTILENA
    a lyrical melody for the voice

CANZONA
    a lyrical song for one or more voices

CASTRATO
    a male singer who combines the vocal range of a boy soprano with the chest and lungs of an adult as a result of deliberate castration. A fascinating sound for audiences, this bizarre practice was known in Italy from the sixteenth through eighteenth centuries

CHORUS
    a musical composition in four or more parts written for a large number of singers; or the large group of singers itself

CLAQUE
    a person or group hired to applaud at a performance, from the French, *claquer*, "to clap"

CLASSICAL
    the period in music from 1750–1850, which was characterized by clarity, symmetry, and formality, especially the Viennese classic school of Haydn, Mozart, Beethoven, and Schubert

CODA
    an additional section at the end of a composition that emphasizes the conclusion

COLORATURA SOPRANO
    the highest range of the female voice, with an agility to perform scales, trills, and embellishments

COMPRIMARIO
    a singer who specializes in the smaller character roles of opera, from the Italian, meaning "next to the first"

CONTRALTO
    the lowest range of the female voice

COUNTERPOINT
    an element in music that consists of two or more lines that sound simultaneously

COUNTERTENOR
    a male singer with an alto range

DECLAMATO
> a style of bombastic singing that demands attention

DIVA
> a female operatic star, from the Italian word for goddess

DRAMATIC SOPRANO
> a high female voice range possessing power and histrionic ability

DYNAMIC MARKS
> the words and signs that indicate intensity of volume. From softest to loudest, the most common are: *pianissimo* (pp), *piano* (p), *mezzo piano* (mp), *mezzo forte* (mf), *forte* (f), and *fortissimo* (ff)

ENSEMBLE
> a piece for more than two singers, such as a duet, trio, quartet, quintet, or sextet

ENTR'ACTE
> an instrumental piece performed between the acts of an opera

FALSETTO
> an artificial technique used by a male singer, particularly tenors, to reach notes above their natural range

FINALE
> the last piece performed in any act of an opera, usually containing contrasting sections

FIORATURA
> ornamentation introduced into a melody, from the Italian *fior*, meaning "flower"

FORTISSIMO see DYNAMIC MARKS

GESAMKUNSTWERK
> the Wagnerian concept of the music drama as a universal art

GRAND OPERA
> an opera that has a serious subject and a fully musicalized text

HARMONY
> the blending of simultaneous sounds of different pitch or quality, making chords; the vertical structure of a musical composition

HELDENTENOR
  a tenor voice with brilliance and great power needed for the "hero" parts, especially in Wagnerian opera

IMPRESSIONISM
  an artistic movement of the late nineteenth and early twentieth centuries as exemplified by the music of Debussy, music that is atmospheric and hints rather than states

INTERMEZZO
  a light and pleasing musical interlude between the acts of an opera

INTERPOLATION
  insertion of additional musical or literary material into a work

INTERVAL
  the distance in pitch between two tones of the musical scale

LEGATO
  sung in a smoothly gliding manner

LEITMOTIV
  a marked melodic phrase (a musical label) that always accompanies the reappearance of a certain person, situation, or abstract idea, especially in Wagner operas

LIBRETTO
  a book containing the words of an opera

LITURGICAL DRAMA
  medieval plays of the twelfth and thirteenth centuries

LYRICS
  the words of a song or an aria

LYRIC SOPRANO
  a high female voice range with a light and pleasant singing style

MADRIGAL
  a type of Italian secular vocal music of the sixteenth century

MAESTRO
  a title for a distinguished teacher, composer, or conductor, from the Italian, meaning "master"

MARKING
  the technique used by a singer to conserve voice and energy by approximating the vocal line and sounds during rehearsal

MASQUE

> a sixteenth- and seventeenth-century entertainment, usually performed at court, combining all the theatrical elements of vocal and instrumental music, dancing, and acting

MASS

> the parts of the ritual church ceremony that are set to music

MELODY

> the combination of successive sounds of various pitch that make up the tune; the horizontal element of a musical composition

MEZZO-SOPRANO

> the middle range of the female voice

MONOPHONIC

> having a single melodic line

MOTET

> a polyphonic musical composition based on a sacred text, usually sung without accompaniment

MUSIC DRAMA

> a play with music; another name for opera

MUSICAL COMEDY

> a comic play in which dialogue is interspersed with songs and dances

NEOCLASSICISM

> a movement in twentieth-century music that includes the reintroduction of styles from the classical period of the seventeenth and eighteenth centuries

OPERA BOUFFE

> operas based on light or sentimental subjects, with happy endings and many comic elements; also known as opera buffa, opéra comique, and comic opera

OPERETTA

> a light entertainment in popular style, with spoken dialogue, music, and dancing

OPUS

> a musical composition; also referring to a composer's works in the chronological order of their issue

ORATORIO
> a composition with a text of religious or contemplative character for solo voices, chorus, and orchestra, performed in a concert hall or church without action, scenery, or costumes

ORCHESTRA PIT
> the lowered area between the stage and the audience that houses the instrumentalists and the conductor

ORCHESTRATION
> the arrangement of music for performance by an orchestra

OVERTURE
> an instrumental composition designed as an introduction to an opera, oratorio, or similar work

PARLANDO
> a direction for the voice to approximate speech, "spoken music," as opposed to the recitative, "musical speech"

PARTITUR
> the conductor's score, which contains all the parts of an orchestral or operatic composition, from the German

PASTICCIO
> an operatic medley with music selected from the works of many composers; a "pasting together," from the Italian word for "pudding"

PIANISSIMO see DYNAMIC MARKS

PITCH
> the placement of a musical sound upon a tonal scale ranging from high to low

PODIUM
> an elevated platform for an orchestra's conductor, from the Greek, meaning "small foot"

POLYPHONIC
> having a simultaneous combination of two or more independent melodic parts

PORTAMENTO
> a smooth and gradual gliding of the voice from one tone to the next through all the intermediate pitches

PRELUDE

> a musical composition that is designed to be used as the introduction to an act of an opera

PREMIERE

> the first public presentation of a work, from the French, meaning "first"

PRIMA DONNA

> a female operatic star or leading lady, from the Italian, meaning "first lady"

PROMPTER'S BOX

> the small housing, downstage center, shielding from the audience's view the person who cues the singers

PROSCENIUM

> in the theater, the area located between the curtain and the orchestra; also the large arch that frames the stage area

RANGE

> the reach of tones within the capacity of a human voice, usually divided into three for the female (soprano, mezzo-soprano, and contralto) and three for the male (tenor, baritone, and bass)

RECITATIVE

> a style of vocal writing designed to simulate the sound of ordinary speech, used in an opera to advance the plot. *Recitativo secco* (dry, or unaccompanied); *recitativo accompagnato* (accompanied)

REGISTER

> in the human voice, the quality of tone color produced according to the placement of sound production, such as *head* tone (highest register of voice), *chest* tone (lowest register of voice), and *throat* tone (middle register)

REPERTORY

> a theatrical company that presents plays or operas from a specified group of works, performed in alternate sequence

REVUE

> a musical show consisting of skits, songs, and dances, often satirizing current events, trends, and personalities

RHYTHM

a regulated pattern formed by a combination of long and short notes

ROMANTICISM

an important movement of the nineteenth century continuing until about 1910, characterized by emotional and subjective qualities in art, and a great freedom of form, as in the works of Berlioz, Mendelssohn, Schumann, and Chopin

RUBINI SOB

named after Giovanni Rubini, a nineteenth-century Italian tenor who used the shake of the voice known as vibrato, producing a musical sob on a prolonged note before the final cadence; also known as the Caruso sob

SCALE

the tonal material of music arranged in a ladder of rising pitches:

a MAJOR SCALE consists of a graduated series of five whole tones and two semitones from the keynote to its octave
a MINOR SCALE consists of five whole tones and two semitones, but in a different order from that of the major scale
a CHROMATIC SCALE consists of all the twelve semitones in a rising order

SCENA

a scene in an opera in which a principal singer commands the stage in a series of musical numbers, from the Italian

SERIAL MUSIC

a term describing some twentieth century compositions distinguished by the absence of traditional rules of tonality, rhythm, melody, and harmony

SINFONIA

an instrumental work of the Italian baroque period composed as an introduction to an opera

SINGSPIEL

a German comic opera resembling the English ballad opera or the French opéra comique in its use of spoken dialogue

SITZPROBE

a German word that refers to a musical rehearsal in which the performers are seated around a piano with scores in hand

SOLFEGE

a singing exercise and teaching method using vowels or sylla-bles (*do, re, mi, fa, sol, la, ti*) for each tone of the scale, from the French

SOPRANO

the highest range of the female voice

SOTTO VOCE

performing with subdued sound, in an undertone, from the Italian, meaning "under the voice"

SOUBRETTE

a female singer who portrays a light comic character, often a ladies' maid involved in intrigue

SPINTO

a category of voice that is pushed toward another category, for example, a "lyrico spinto"—a light lyric voice pushed to in-clude the dramatic range, from the Italian, *spingere*, meaning "to push"

SPRECHSTIMME

a style of voice production that lies between song and speech, from the German meaning "speaking voice"

STACCATO

a direction to perform the notes of a passage in a short, dis-tinct, and often pointed manner, from the Italian

STAGE DIRECTIONS

Stage right is the area at the performer's right, viewed by the audience as the left side of the stage; the reverse applies to *Stage left*. Considering that early stages were built on a slight angle or rake, the farthest from the audience is *Upstage*, and the closest is *Downstage*

SUPERNUMERARY

an extra actor who is employed to appear in a crowd scene or a spectacle; commonly called a "super"

TEMPO

the speed of a composition, ranging from very slow (*largo*) to very fast (*prestissimo*)

TENOR

the highest natural male voice range

TESSITURA
> the general range of a vocal part, whether high or low in its average pitch, from the Italian word for texture

TONALITY
> the principle of key in music, giving the composition a base, or center

TRAGEDIE LYRIQUE
> a seventeenth-century French theatrical entertainment that featured ballet, song, and lavish spectacle

TREMOLO
> excessive vibrations in a voice that push it out of control

TRILL
> the rapid alternation of two adjacent notes

VAUDEVILLE
> short comedies interspersed with popular songs

VERISMO
> an Italian operatic style of the late nineteenth century using a realistic subject from everyday life for the plot

VIBRATO
> a vibration in the voice which, in moderation, adds to the emotional beauty of the tone

VOCAL CORDS
> the lower of two pairs of bands or folds in the larynx that vibrate when pulled together and when air is passed up from the lungs, producing vocal sounds

WINGS
> the unseen offstage areas on either side of the stage

V
DISCOGRAPHY

The following are some of the author's suggested audiodiscs which are currently available. Listed in addition to the composer and the title of the opera are the principal singers, the conductor, the orchestra, and the label and catalog number of the recording.

BELLINI   *NORMA*
   Sutherland, Horne, Alexander, Cross
   Bonynge and the London Symphony
   LONDON 1394 (3 records)

BERNSTEIN   *CANDIDE*
   Cook, Rounseville, Adrian, Petina
   Krachmalnick and original cast orchestra
   COLUMBIA OS2350 (1 record)

BIZET   *CARMEN*
   Horne, Maliponte, McCracken, Krause
   Bernstein and the Metropolitan Opera Orchestra
   DEUTSCHE GRAMMOPHON 2709043 (3 records)

BRITTEN   *PETER GRIMES*
   Harper, Vickers, Summers
   Davis and the Royal Opera Orchestra
   PHILIPS 6769014 (3 records)

DONIZETTI   *LUCIA DI LAMMERMOOR*
   Callas, Tagliavini, Cappuccilli
   Serafin and the Philharmonia Orchestra
   Angel S3601 (2 records)

GERSHWIN   *PORGY AND BESS*
Dale, Albert, Smith
De Main and the Houston Grand Opera
RCA ARL3-2109 (3 records)

GOUNOD   *FAUST*
De los Angeles, Gedda, Christoff
Cluytens and the Paris Opera Orchestra
ANGEL S3622 (4 records)

HANDEL   *JULIUS CAESAR*
Sills, Wolff, Forrester, Treigle
Rudel and the New York City Opera
RCA LSC6182 (3 records)

HUMPERDINCK   *HANSEL AND GRETEL*
Popp, Fassbaender, Hamari, Berry
Solti and the Vienna Philharmonic
LONDON 12112 (2 records)

LEHAR   *THE MERRY WIDOW*
Schwarzkopf, Gedda, Loose, Kunz
Ackermann and the Philharmonia Orchestra
ANGEL S3630 (2 records)

LEONCAVALLO   *I PAGLIACCI*
Caballé, Domingo, Milnes
Santi and the London Symphony
RCA LSC7090 (2 records)

MASCAGNI   *CAVALLERIA RUSTICANA*
De los Angeles, Corelli, Sereni
Santini and the Rome Opera
ANGEL S3632 (2 records)

MOZART   *COSÌ FAN TUTTE*
Schwarzkopf, Ludwig, Kraus, Berry
Böhm and the Philharmonia Orchestra
ANGEL S3631 (4 records)

DON GIOVANNI
Nilsson, Arroyo, Talvela, Fischer-Dieskau
Böhm and the Prague National Theater Orchestra
DEUTSCHE GRAMMOPHON 2711006 (4 records)

THE MARRIAGE OF FIGARO
Norman, Freni, Minton, Wixell
Davis and the BBC Symphony Orchestra
PHILIPS 6707014 (4 records)

OFFENBACH   THE TALES OF HOFFMANN
Sutherland, Tourangeau, Domingo, Cuenod
Bonynge and the Suisse Romande
LONDON OSA13106 (3 records)

PONCHIELLI   LA GIOCONDA
Callas, Cossotto, Ferraro, Cappuccilli
Votto and the orchestra of La Scala
SERAPHIM S6031 (3 records)

PUCCINI   LA BOHÈME
Freni, Harwood, Pavarotti, Panerai, Ghiaurov
Karajan and the Berlin Philharmonic
LONDON OSA1299 (2 records)

PUCCINI   MADAMA BUTTERFLY
Price, Tucker
Leinsdorf and the Italian Opera Orchestra
RCA LSC6160 (3 records)

TOSCA
Callas, Bergonzi, Gobbi
Prêtre and the Paris Opera Orchestra
ANGEL S3655 (2 records)

ROSSINI   THE BARBER OF SEVILLE
Sills, Barbieri, Gedda, Milnes, Raimondi
Levine and the London Symphony
ANGEL SX3761 (3 records)

SONDHEIM   SWEENEY TODD
Lansbury, Cariou
Gemignani and original cast orchestra
RCA CBL3379 (2 records)

STRAUSS, J.   DIE FLEDERMAUS
Rothenberger, Fassbaender, Gedda, Berry
Boskovsky and the Vienna Symphony
ANGEL S3790 (2 records)

STRAUSS, R.   *DER ROSENKAVALIER*
Ludwig, Jones, Popp, Berry
Bernstein and the Vienna Philharmonic
COLUMBIA D4M30652 (4 records)

SULLIVAN   *IOLANTHE*
D'Oyly Carte Opera Company
Nash and the Royal Philharmonic
LONDON OSA12104 (2 records)

VERDI   *AIDA*
Price, Bumbry, Domingo, Milnes, Raimondi
Leinsdorf and the London Symphony
RCA LSC6198 (3 records)

FALSTAFF
Ligabue, Sciutti, Resnik, Fischer-Dieskau
Bernstein and the Vienna Philharmonic
COLUMBIA D3S750 (3 records)

LA TRAVIATA
Albanese, Peerce, Merrill
Toscanini and the NBC Symphony
RCA VICTOR LM6003 (2 records)

IL TROVATORE
Price, Cossotto, Domingo, Milnes
Mehta and the New Philharmonia
RCA LSC6194 (3 records)

WAGNER   *DIE MEISTERSINGER*
Donath, Kollo, Schreier, Evans, Adam
Karajan and the Dresden State Opera
ANGEL S3776 (5 records)

INDEX